the *Vegetarian Student* cookbook

GREAT GRUB FOR THE HUNGRY AND THE BROKE

RYLAND
PETERS
& SMALL
LONDON NEW YORK

Senior Designer Iona Hoyle

Senior Editor Céline Hughes

Picture Research Emily Westlake

Production Controller Maria Petalidou

Art Director Leslie Harrington

Publishing Director Alison Starling

Indexer Penelope Kent

First published in the UK in 2010
by Ryland Peters & Small
20–21 Jockey's Fields
London WC1R 4BW
www.rylandpeters.com

10 9 8 7 6 5 4 3 2 1

Text © Nadia Arumugam, Fiona Beckett, Vatcharin
Bhumichitr, Celia Brooks Brown, Tamsin Burnett-Hall, Maxine
Clark, Linda Collister, Ross Dobson, Ursula Ferrigno, Liz
Franklin, Clare Ferguson, Manisha Gambhir Harkins, Tonia
George, Brian Glover, Nicola Graimes, Kate Habershon,
Rachael Anne Hill, Caroline Marson, Jane Noraika, Louise
Pickford, Rena Salaman, Jennie Shapter, Fiona Smith, Sonia
Stevenson, Sunil Vijayakar, Fran Warde, Laura Washburn,
Lindy Wildsmith, and Ryland Peters & Small 2010

Design and photographs © Ryland Peters & Small 2010

ISBN: 978-1-84975-018-9

The recipes in this book have been published previously
by Ryland Peters & Small.

Printed and bound in China

A CIP record for this book is available from
the British Library.

Notes:

• All spoon measurements are level, unless
otherwise specified.

• Ovens should be preheated to the specified
temperature. Recipes in this book were tested using
a regular oven. If using a fan-assisted oven, follow
the manufacturer's instructions for adjusting
temperatures.

• All eggs are medium, unless otherwise specified.
Recipes containing raw or partially cooked egg,
or raw fish or shellfish, should not be served to the
very young, very old, anyone with a compromised
immune system or pregnant women.

contents

Now that you're a fully fledged student and embracing independence, you're going to want to know how to cook up a storm in the kitchen. *The Vegetarian Student Cookbook* is here to allay any fears you might have about cooking veggie food for yourself. Some of the recipes are super-quick, while others need time to work their magic. Either way, they are stress-free and designed to satisfy, whether you're coming home late with a mammoth hunger after a night out, or you're having friends over for a lazy Sunday lunch. You'll soon realize that veggie food isn't dull or time-consuming and that there are lots of easy and tasty dishes you can whip up. Check out the tips in the first few pages before you get started – they will make life a lot easier and ensure that your culinary efforts are always successful, undaunting, and above all, fun.

introduction

kitchen know-how

The recipes in this book need the minimum of kitchen equipment. Some recipes, like the desserts, will require extras, e.g. a handheld electric whisk (which can be bought very cheaply), a baking tin for brownies, etc. but you can go a long way with these essentials:

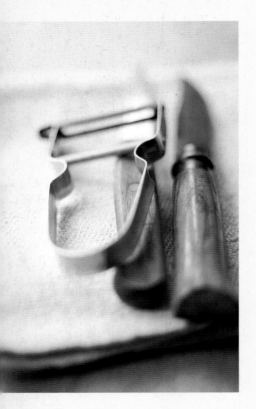

2 or 3 sharp knives, including a serrated knife

wooden spoon

fish/egg slice

potato masher

garlic crusher

pepper mill

tin opener

vegetable peeler

cheese grater

2 chopping boards (1 for meat-eating friends to use and 1 for veg)

large mixing bowl

sieve

colander

1 large and 1 medium saucepan

frying pan with a lid

baking tray

roasting tin

ovenproof dish (Pyrex or ceramic)

measuring jug

weighing scales

a selection of airtight containers

kettle

toaster

aluminium foil

clingfilm

greaseproof paper

kitchen paper

cleaning stuff, including washing up liquid, sponges and surface cleaner

tea towels

oven gloves

Every recipe has at least one of these symbols:

 This tells you roughly how many people the recipe should serve.

 This is an extra-quick recipe, and shouldn't take you longer than 20 minutes once you've prepared the ingredients.

Additionally, where a recipe calls for salt and black pepper, use sea salt and freshly ground black pepper if at all possible. They give the best flavour.

Whenever a recipe calls for olive oil, if you are using it raw (e.g. in a salad dressing or drizzled over vegetables), the extra virgin variety is the tastiest. For frying or roasting, use a basic (not extra virgin), mild variety.

Whenever a recipe calls for zest from a citrus fruit, try to buy the fruit unwaxed, so that you are not consuming the chemicals sprayed onto the fruit peel. However, if you can't find unwaxed or it is too expensive, wash the waxed fruit in hot water before you use it.

handy ingredients

sea salt

black peppercorns

olive oil

vegetable or
sunflower oil

balsamic vinegar

red or white wine
vinegar

dark or light soy sauce

tomato ketchup (as if
you needed reminding!)

mustard

mayonnaise

long grain rice

risotto rice

dried pasta,
including spaghetti

couscous

vegetable stock cubes
or bouillon powder

tinned chopped
tomatoes

a selection of tinned
beans, such as
cannellini, kidney

plain flour

sugar

tomato purée

a selection of dried
herbs, such as oregano

a selection of dried
spices, such as curry
powder, ground cumin,
paprika, chilli powder
or dried red chilli flakes

dried porcini
mushrooms

Marmite

honey

butter or margarine

milk

onions

garlic

food safety

• The first rule of cooking is to always keep your kitchen clean! Keep it tidy and disinfect worktops after use with a mild detergent or an antibacterial cleaner. Keep pets off surfaces and, as far as possible, keep them out of the kitchen.

• Store food safely to avoid cross-contamination. Keep food in clean, dry, airtight containers, always store raw and cooked foods separately and wash utensils (and your hands) between preparing raw and cooked foods.

• Wash your hands well with hot, soapy water before and after handling food.

• Never put hot food into a fridge, as this will increase the internal temperature to an unsafe level. Cool leftover food quickly to room temperature, ideally by transferring it to a cold dish, then refrigerate. Cool large dishes such as stews by putting the dish in a sink of cold water. Stir occasionally (change the water often to keep the temperature low), then refrigerate once cool. During cooling, cover the food loosely with clingfilm to protect it from contamination.

• Don't use perishable food beyond the 'use-by' date as it could be a health risk. If you have any doubts about the food, discard it.

• Reheated food must be piping hot throughout before consumption. Never reheat any type of food more than once.

• If you are going to freeze food, freeze food that is in prime condition, on the day of purchase, or as soon as a dish is made and cooled. Freeze it quickly and in small quantities, if possible. Label and date food and keep a good rotation of stock in the freezer.

• Always leave a gap in the container when freezing liquids, so that there is enough room for the liquid to expand as it freezes.

• Always let food cool before freezing it. Warm or hot food will increase the internal temperature of the freezer and may cause other foods to begin to defrost and spoil.

• Use proper oven gloves to remove hot dishes from the oven – don't just use a tea towel because you risk burning yourself. Tea towels are also a breeding ground for germs so only use them for drying, and wash them often.

• Hard cheeses such as Cheddar, Gruyère and Parmesan will keep for up to 3 weeks if stored correctly. Once opened, fresh, soft cheeses such as cream cheese should be consumed within 3 days.

• Wash hands before and after handling eggs, and discard any cracked and/or dirty eggs.

• If your kitchen is prone to over-heating, it is best to store eggs in their box in the fridge. Keep them pointed-end downwards and away from strong-smelling foods, as they can absorb odours. Always use by the 'best-before' date.

• Leftover tinned foods should be transferred to an airtight container, kept in the fridge and eaten within 2 days. Once tins are opened, the contents should be treated as fresh food. This doesn't apply to food sold in tubs with resealable lids, such as cocoa powder.

• Cooked rice is a potential source of food poisoning. Cool leftovers quickly (ideally within an hour), then store in an airtight container in the fridge and use within 24 hours. Always reheat cooked cold rice until piping hot.

• The natural oils in chillies may cause irritation to your skin and eyes. When preparing them, wear disposable gloves or pull a small polythene bag over each hand, secured with an elastic band around the wrist, to create a glove.

ingredients tips

• Chop leftover fresh herbs, spoon them into an ice-cube tray, top with a little water and freeze. Once solid, put the cubes in a freezer bag. Seal, label and return to the freezer. Add the frozen herb cubes to soups, casseroles and sauces.

• When substituting dried herbs for fresh, use roughly half the quantity the recipe calls for, as dried herbs have a more concentrated flavour.

• The colour of a fresh chilli is no indication of how hot it will be. Generally speaking, the smaller and thinner the chilli, the hotter it will be.

• To reduce the heat of a fresh chilli, cut it in half lengthways, then scrape out and discard the seeds and membranes (or core). See also 'food safety' above for advice on handling chillies.

• Most vegetables keep best in the fridge, but a cool, dark place is also good if you lack fridge space. Potatoes should always be stored in the dark, otherwise they go green or sprout, making them inedible.

• To skin tomatoes, score a cross in the base of each one using a sharp knife. Put them in a heatproof bowl, cover with boiling water, leave for about 30 seconds, then transfer them to a bowl of cold water. When cool enough to handle, drain and peel off the skins with a knife.

• To clean leeks, trim them, then slit them lengthways about a third of the way through. Open the leaves a little and wash away any dirt from between the layers under cold running water.

• Store coffee (beans and ground) in the fridge or freezer, or it will go stale very quickly.

• Store flour in its original sealed packaging or in an airtight container in a cool, dry, airy place. Ideally, buy and store small quantities at a time, to help avoid infestation of psocids (very small, barely visible, grey-brown insects), which may appear even in the cleanest of homes. If you do find these small insects in your flour, dispose of it immediately and wash and dry the container thoroughly. Never mix new flour with old.

• If you run out of self-raising flour, sift together 2 teaspoons of baking powder with every 225 g plain flour. This will not be quite as effective but it is a good emergency substitute.

• Store oils, well sealed, in a cool, dark, dry place, away from direct sunlight. They can be kept in the fridge (though this is not necessary), but oils such as olive oil tend to solidify and go cloudy in the fridge. If this happens, bring the oil back to room temperature before use.

• Small pasta tubes and twists such as penne and fusilli are good for chunky vegetable sauces and some cream-based sauces. Smooth, creamy, butter- or olive oil-based sauces are ideal for long strands such as spaghetti (so the sauce can cling to the pasta).

• Dried pasta has a long shelf life and should be stored in its unopened packet or in an airtight container in a cool, dry place.

Leftover cooked pasta should be kept in a sealed container in the fridge and used within 2 days. Ordinary cooked pasta does not freeze well on its own, but it freezes successfully in dishes such as lasagne and cannelloni. Allow 85–115 g dried pasta per person.

• Pasta must be cooked in a large volume of salted, boiling water. Keep the water at a rolling boil throughout cooking. Once you have added the pasta to the boiling water, give it a stir, then cover the pan to help the water return to the boil as quickly as possible. Remove the lid once the water has started boiling again (to prevent the water boiling over), and stir occasionally. Check the instructions on the packet for cooking times. When it is ready, cooked pasta should be al dente – tender but still with a slight resistance.

• As an accompaniment, allow 55–85 g uncooked rice per person or for a main like risotto, up to 115 g.

• Rice may be rinsed before cooking to remove tiny pieces of grit or excess starch. Most packaged rice is checked and clean, however, so rinsing it is unnecessary and will wash away nutrients. Risotto rice is not washed before use, but basmati rice usually is – rinse it under cold water until the water runs clear.

taste tips

• Try mixing a pinch or two of ground spices such as curry powder, chilli powder or turmeric with breadcrumbs or flour, and use to coat foods before frying. Add ground spices such as cinnamon, mixed spice or ginger to fruit crumble toppings. A pinch or two of grated nutmeg will perk up mashed potatoes, cheese sauce, cooked spinach, bread sauce and rice puddings.

• Stir wholegrain mustard into mashed potatoes or mayonnaise before serving to add extra flavour. Mustard also enhances salad dressings and sauces. A pinch of mustard powder added to cheese dishes will enhance the flavour.

• If you add too much salt to a soup or casserole, add one or two peeled and cubed potatoes to soak up the salt, cooking until tender. Discard the potatoes before serving.

• An excellent way of thickening soups is to stir in a little oatmeal. It adds flavour and richness too. A small amount of instant mashed potato stirred in at the last minute is also a good way of thickening soup.

• Add a little pearl barley to soups and stews – it will add flavour and texture and have a thickening effect.

• A teaspoon or two of pesto sauce stirred into each portion of a hot vegetable soup just before serving will liven it up.

• For a tasty and creamy salad dressing, mash some blue cheese and stir it into mayonnaise, or a mixture of mayonnaise and natural Greek yoghurt.

• Add some health and a satisfying crunch to salads by tossing in a handful or two of lightly toasted seeds or chopped nuts just before serving. Good ideas include sunflower, sesame or pumpkin seeds and hazelnuts, walnuts, pecan nuts or pistachios. Toasted seeds can also be sprinkled over cooked vegetables.

• If you over-cook an omelette, leave it to cool and use it as a sandwich filling. Chop the omelette and combine it with mayonnaise and snipped chives, if you like.

- Bulk out a pasta or rice salad by adding a tin of drained and rinsed beans such as chickpeas, red kidney beans or black-eye beans.
- For an extra-crunchy crumble topping, replace 25 g of the flour with the same weight of chopped nuts, rolled oats or oatmeal, or replace caster sugar with granulated or Demerara sugar.

kitchen wisdom

- To remove odours from a container that you want to use again, fill the container with hot water, then stir in 1 tablespoon baking powder. Leave it to stand overnight, then wash, rinse well and dry before use.
- If you transfer foods from packets to storage containers, sellotape the food label onto the container so you can easily identify its contents and you have a record of the manufacturer's cooking instructions, if necessary. Make a note of the 'best-before' or 'use-by' date on the container, too.
- For convenient single servings, freeze portions of home-made soup in large, thick paper cups or small individual containers. Remove them from the freezer as required, defrost and reheat the soup thoroughly before serving.
- To make salad dressings or vinaigrettes, put all the ingredients in a clean screw-top jar, seal and shake well. Alternatively, put the ingredients straight into the salad bowl and whisk together well, before adding the salad.
- Spirits with an alcohol content of 35% or over can be kept in the freezer – this is ideal for those which should be served ice-cold.

microwave safety

- The more food you are cooking, and the colder it is, the longer it will take to cook in a microwave.
- Metal containers, china with a metallic trim, foil or crystal glass (which contains lead) should not be used in a microwave. Metal reflects microwaves and may damage the oven components. Microwave-safe plastic containers, ovenproof glass and ceramic dishes are all suitable, as is most household glazed china. Paper plates and kitchen paper can be used to reheat food for short periods. Roasting bags (pierced) may be used in a microwave.
- Many foods need to be covered during microwaving. Use microwave-safe clingfilm, a plate or a lid. Pierce clingfilm, or leave a gap at one side if using a plate or lid, to allow excess steam to escape.
- Use a microwave with a built-in turntable if possible, and make sure that you stir the food several times during cooking to ensure even cooking throughout. The food on the outer edges usually cooks first.

- Never operate a microwave when it is empty, as the microwaves will bounce back to and damage the oven components.
- Be careful when stirring heated liquids in a container in the microwave, as they can bubble up without warning.
- After food has been removed from the microwave, it will continue to cook due to the residual heat within the food, so adhere to standing times when they are given in recipes.
- Take care when removing the cover from a microwave container as the steam inside will be very hot.

light bites and sides

spicy lentil dip

spicy *lentil* dip

Lentils contain loads of great things – protein, fibre, zinc and more – and they are also very filling, so they make an ideal base for a snack or meal. Serve with crudités or pita bread.

serves 6

Put the lentils and 400 ml water in a saucepan. Bring to the boil, reduce the heat and simmer for 20–30 minutes, until the water is absorbed. Remove from the heat and mash with a fork.

Melt the butter in a small saucepan, add the onion and cook gently for about 5 minutes, until soft but not coloured. Add the curry powder and cook for a further 1–2 minutes. Add the mashed lentils to the pan, stir and cook for 5 minutes more. Season with salt and pepper.

Remove the pan from the heat. If the dip is a bit dry, add a couple of teaspoons of water to moisten. Alternatively, for a chunkier texture, leave the mixture as it is.

Leave to cool. Sprinkle with coriander, if using, and serve with your choice of vegetable crudités and strips of pita bread.

125 g red lentils

25 g butter

1 small onion, finely chopped

1–2 tablespoons curry powder

salt and black pepper

freshly chopped coriander, to serve (optional)

avocado salsa

Serve this salsa as a dip with crudités, toasted pita bread or crisps – it's much better than any guacamole you can buy ready-made. To check whether the avocado is ripe, take the fruit in your hand and press gently at the neck end – if it is in peak condition, it will give a little without being too soft.

serves 4–6

Combine all the ingredients in a bowl and season to taste. Cover and set aside to infuse for 15 minutes, then serve immediately as the salsa will start to discolour after 30 minutes.

2 ripe avocados, peeled, stoned and diced

1 garlic clove, crushed

1 large red chilli, deseeded and finely chopped

2 tomatoes, deseeded and diced

2 tablespoons olive oil

2 tablespoons freshly chopped coriander

juice of ½ lime

salt and black pepper

chilli and mint raita

a large handful of mint

1 teaspoon salt

½ teaspoon sugar

250 ml natural yoghurt

1 green chilli, finely sliced
(optional)

 serves 2–3

 Q

Yoghurt and mint are a common combination in India, often used to temper hot, spicy dishes. But with its own chilli kick (optional) and some warm naan bread, this makes a great dip.

Very finely chop the mint leaves and put in a bowl with the salt, sugar and yoghurt and mix well. Serve sprinkled with the sliced green chilli, if using, and some warm naan bread.

tomato, onion and chilli raita

250 ml natural yoghurt

1 teaspoon salt

1 teaspoon sugar

juice of ½ lemon

1 red onion, finely diced

1 tomato, deseeded
and chopped

5 cm cucumber, deseeded
and chopped

1 red chilli, chopped

1 green chilli, chopped

 serves 2–3

This combination of tomato, onion and chilli makes a great salsa by itself, but when mixed with yoghurt, it's creamy and delicious. Serve with warm naan bread.

Put the yoghurt, salt, sugar and lemon juice in a bowl and mix to dissolve the sugar. Add the onion, tomato, cucumber and chillies and stir gently. Refrigerate for 30 minutes, then serve with some warn naan bread.

cucumber and ginger raita

250 ml natural yoghurt

2 cm fresh ginger, peeled
and grated

1 teaspoon salt

1 tablespoon sugar

1 tablespoon lemon juice

½ teaspoon ground turmeric

5 cm cucumber

 serves 2–3

Serve this raita with a hot curry – cucumber and yoghurt are known to help cool the effect of chillies.

Put the yoghurt, ginger, salt, sugar, lemon juice and turmeric into a bowl and mix to dissolve the sugar.

Cut the cucumber in half lengthways and scrape out the seeds with a teaspoon. If the skin is tough or waxed, peel it off: otherwise leave it on. Cut the cucumber into matchstick strips, put into a bowl and pour over the yoghurt dressing. Refrigerate for 30 minutes, then serve.

Note See bottom picture on page 17 for photograph of all three raitas.

baba ganoush

baba ganoush

Baba ganoush is a famous Middle-Eastern creamy aubergine purée with smoky overtones. Serve it as a dip or as a side dish.

serves
8

Q

Using a pair of heatproof tongs, very carefully hold the aubergines over the open gas flame on top of the stove and cook until well charred on all sides. The steam created inside the vegetable will cook the flesh. The aubergines must be charred all over and soft in the middle. Remove from the flame and leave on a plate until cool enough to handle.

Carefully pull off the skins and stems. Don't leave any charred bits. Put the flesh into a bowl, then mash with a potato masher: the texture should not be too smooth. Add the yoghurt, tahini, garlic and salt and mash again.

Add the juice of 1 lemon, taste, then gradually add more juice until you achieve flavour and texture to your taste. Transfer to a bowl and sprinkle with parsley, if using. Serve with wedges of toasted pita bread.

3 aubergines

4 tablespoons plain yoghurt

2 tablespoons tahini (sesame seed paste)

1 garlic clove, crushed

1 teaspoon salt

juice of 1–2 lemons, to taste

1 tablespoon freshly chopped parsley (optional)

*portobello mushrooms
with lemon and olive oil*

portobello *mushrooms* with *lemon* and *olive oil*

The earthy, almost meaty flavour of portobello mushrooms needs very little to improve it. Serve this as a simple, but tasty, snack when friends are round and complaining about being hungry.

serves
4

4 large portobello mushrooms, about 250 g

Marinade

2 tablespoons olive oil

1 tablespoon soy sauce

grated zest and juice of 1 lemon

2 garlic cloves, crushed

4 sprigs of rosemary

black pepper

To make the marinade, put the olive oil, soy sauce, lemon zest and juice, garlic, rosemary and some pepper in a bowl, mix well, then pour over the mushrooms so that they are well covered. Set aside to infuse for 30 minutes.

Put a griddle pan or frying pan over medium heat to preheat. Put the mushrooms in the pan and cook for 5 minutes on each side or until softened.

Serve the mushrooms on top of a thick slice of toast and pour any remaining marinade juices over the top.

olive oil and *garlic* bread

This is a dairy-free version of everyone's guilty pleasure: garlic bread. Use sea salt flakes if you can, as they add texture. If you only have fine salt, reduce the quantity to ¼ teaspoon.

serves
6–8

Q

1 baguette (French stick)

4 tablespoons olive oil

4 garlic cloves, crushed

½ teaspoon sea salt flakes

Preheat the oven to 200°C (400°F) Gas 6.

Slice the baguette on the diagonal at 3-cm intervals, but do not cut all the way through to the base. Put on a long piece of aluminium foil.

In a small bowl, combine the oil, garlic and salt. Using a spoon, drizzle a little of the garlic oil between each slice of baguette, then brush the remaining garlic oil over the top. Wrap in the foil.

Bake in the preheated oven for 10 minutes until hot through. Serve the bread immediately.

minty char-grilled *courgettes*

4 courgettes, about 1 kg

2 tablespoons olive oil

4 teaspoons white wine vinegar

a handful of mint, leaves torn

salt and black pepper

Perfect for the summer, this Mediterranean recipe and simple char-grilling technique bring out the best in courgettes. Serve as a side dish or as a light lunch with another salad.

Trim and discard the ends of the courgettes, then cut the vegetable lengthways into ribbon-like slices and put in a bowl. Drizzle with the olive oil and, using your hands, gently toss the slices until well coated.

Preheat a griddle pan or non-stick frying pan over high heat until very hot. Add the courgette ribbons (in batches, if necessary) and cook until softened and marked with black stripes on both sides. Transfer to a shallow dish and drizzle with the vinegar while the courgettes are still warm. Add salt and pepper and leave to cool.

Pile the courgette ribbons into a bowl, sprinkle with the mint and add lots more black pepper. Serve immediately.

scrambled *eggs* with *mushrooms*

250 g portobello mushrooms, or mixed wild mushrooms

6 eggs

50 g butter

2 teaspoons freshly chopped thyme

salt and black pepper

Add some sautéed mushrooms to scrambled eggs on toast and you've got yourself the perfect no-fuss snack for two, no matter what time of day it is.

Wipe the mushrooms with a damp cloth and cut into thick slices. Put the eggs in a bowl, add salt and pepper and whisk until blended.

Melt 40 g of the butter in a large frying pan. As soon as it stops foaming, add the mushrooms, thyme, salt and pepper. Fry over medium heat until lightly browned and the juices are starting to run.

Push the mushrooms to one side of the pan, add the remaining butter, then pour in the beaten eggs, stirring with a fork until almost set.

Gradually stir in the mushrooms from the sides of the pan, cook a moment longer and spoon onto toast to serve.

*minty char-grilled
courgettes*

beef tomatoes with garlic and herb butter

baked fennel with shallots and spicy dressing

beef tomatoes with *garlic* and *herb* butter

serves 4

These are so easy to make, but beware that they need over an hour in the oven to bake to perfection. They would make a good, stress-free side dish for a special dinner, but they're also a great choice for an everyday meal for two.

4 beef tomatoes

3 garlic cloves, crushed

70 g butter, softened

1 teaspoon chilli oil (optional)

a large handful of parsley, freshly chopped

black pepper

olive oil, for sprinkling

Preheat the oven to 150°C (300°F) Gas 2.

Remove the stalk from each tomato and carefully cut out a small cavity for the filling.

Put the garlic, butter, chilli oil, if using, parsley and some pepper in a bowl and mix well. Fill the tomato cavities with the garlic mixture, pressing down gently as you go. Put on a baking tray, sprinkle with olive oil and roast in the preheated oven for 1 hour 20 minutes.

Eat hot from the oven with some of the cooking juices poured over the top.

baked *fennel* with *shallots* and spicy dressing

Fennel is a fantastic vegetable to have in your cooking repertoire because it's so versatile. You can roast it with other vegetables or serve it raw in a salad, thinly sliced or chopped. This is the kind of recipe that could serve up to 8 people as a small side, or far fewer as the main component of a meal.

serves
6–8

Preheat the oven to 170°C (325°F) Gas 3.

Cut the base off the fennel bulbs and trim the tops. Cut each bulb lengthways into 4 and cut out the hard core. Put in an ovenproof dish and add the shallots, sugar and 2 tablespoons of the olive oil. Mix well and bake in the preheated oven for 30 minutes.

Put the remaining olive oil in a small saucepan, add the garlic and ginger and cook over very low heat for 10 minutes. Add the spring onions, sesame oil, lemon juice, chilli powder and salt and pepper to taste. Gently bring to a simmer, then pour over the roasted fennel. Mix and serve with the juices.

2 fennel bulbs

4 shallots, chopped

1 teaspoon sugar

3 tablespoons olive oil

1 garlic clove, crushed

2.5 cm fresh ginger, peeled and chopped

a bunch of spring onions, sliced

1 tablespoon sesame oil

juice of 1 lemon

½ teaspoon chilli powder

salt and black pepper

mozzarella and *basil* toasties

These cheesy snacks are great with beer or a glass of white wine if you've got friends over for the evening.

makes
16

Trim any thick crusts off the bread. Lay 4 slices of the bread on a work surface and divide the mozzarella and basil on top. Top each with a slice of bread.

Preheat a large, non-stick frying pan over medium heat and add half of the olive oil. Sit the sandwiches in the pan and drizzle the remaining oil on the top slices of bread.

Cook for 2–3 minutes, using a spatula to gently press down on the sandwiches. Turn over and cook for a further 2 minutes. Transfer to a chopping board and cut each sandwich into 4 fingers. Season with a little salt and pepper and serve immediately while the mozzarella is still molten.

8 thin slices of white bread

200 g mozzarella

a handful of basil, leaves torn

4 tablespoons olive oil

salt and black pepper

*whole cauliflower
with olives*

whole *cauliflower* with *olives*

This is such an impressive way to serve a whole creamy head of cauliflower – let your friends help themselves, pulling out the florets. It would complement a risotto nicely.

serves
4

1 large whole cauliflower, green leaves removed and reserved

2 onions, finely chopped

300 g small, stoned green olives, sliced

6 tablespoons olive oil, plus extra to serve

a handful of parsley, freshly chopped, to serve

salt

Line a large, heavy-based saucepan with the reserved outer leaves from the cauliflower. Put the cauliflower on top. Sprinkle with the onion, olives and some salt, then pour over the olive oil. Cover with a lid, set over the lowest heat and cook gently for about 40 minutes or until tender – there should be no resistance when a fork is inserted into the middle of the cauliflower.

Carefully lift the cauliflower out of the saucepan and onto a large plate – be very careful not to break it. Pile the onion and olives on top, then sprinkle with the parsley and more olive oil and serve.

creamy *spinach*

Steamed spinach is fine when you need a quick side vegetable but try this creamy spinach for something a bit more special.

serves
4

Q

500 g fresh spinach

2 tablespoons crème fraîche

grated nutmeg (optional)

Discard any hard central stalks from the spinach and wash the leaves thoroughly in plenty of cold water. Drain well, then put the spinach in a large saucepan with only the water left clinging to the leaves. Cook for 2–3 minutes until wilted. Drain well, squeezing out any excess water. Chop finely.

Return the spinach to the rinsed pan and add 1 teaspoon water and the crème fraîche. Heat over medium heat for 1 minute, stirring. Serve immediately, sprinkled with a little grated nutmeg, if using.

smashed roast *potatoes*

16 small new potatoes

2 tablespoons olive oil

1 teaspoon salt

1–2 sprigs of rosemary
(optional)

serves
4

You will need tiny little new potatoes to make perfect smashed roast spuds. The initial blast of a really hot oven is what makes the potatoes so soft and fluffy on the inside and about to burst out of their crispy little skins. This is a novel and highly effective way to roast potatoes so be warned, it's likely you may not go back to the old way of roasting after you try this!

Preheat the oven to 230°C (450°F) Gas 8 and put a non-stick (if possible) roasting tin in the oven to heat up for 10 minutes.

Put the potatoes in a bowl with 1 tablespoon of the oil and toss to coat in the oil. Put the potatoes in the hot tin and roast in the preheated oven for 20 minutes.

Remove the roasting tin from the oven and turn the potatoes over. Gently press down on each potato with the back of large metal spoon until you hear the potato skin pop.

Drizzle the remaining oil over the potatoes, sprinkle with the salt and throw in the rosemary, if using. Return to the oven for a further 10 minutes, until the potatoes are crispy and golden.

lemon roast *potato* wedges

4 potatoes, each cut into
8 wedges

juice of ½ lemon

1–2 tablespoons olive oil

salt and black pepper

serves
4

Your very own, fancy oven chips. Serve with a veggie pie and peas and you've made pub grub without even leaving the house!

Preheat the oven to 220°C (425°F) Gas 7.

Put the potato wedges in a non-stick (if possible) roasting tin, add the lemon juice and season with salt and pepper. Drizzle with the olive oil and stir well. Cook in the preheated oven for 20–30 minutes until crisp and golden, turning once or twice. Transfer to a serving dish and serve.

Variation When the potatoes are ready, add 250 g cherry tomatoes pricked with the point of a knife, then stir into the potatoes and return to the oven for 5 minutes or until the tomato skins start to split.

smashed roast potatoes

portuguese potatoes

portuguese *potatoes*

These are very similar to the Smashed Roast Potatoes on page 30, but they are cooked on the hob instead of in the oven, and they contain a generous amount of garlic – so these are only for very keen garlic lovers!

serves 6

4 tablespoons olive oil

1.5 kg small waxy new potatoes

6 garlic cloves, crushed

3 sprigs of rosemary

2 teaspoons sea salt flakes (or fine sea salt)

Heat the oil in a large, heavy-based saucepan set over medium heat. Add the potatoes. Add the garlic to the oil and potatoes along with the rosemary and salt. Stir well, reduce the heat to low, then cover and cook for 50–60 minutes for walnut-sized potatoes or 1–1¼ hours for egg-sized ones, stirring occasionally.

Note These Portuguese-style potatoes are also delicious as a cold side dish. You can make them the day before, and once cool, cover and refrigerate. Bring back to room temperature for 1 hour before serving.

crushed *peas*

Peas are always a great standby side dish because you're bound to have a bag in the freezer! They also have the added bonus of being delicious and making a good accompaniment to most food.

serves 3

Q

1 tablespoon olive oil

½ onion, thinly sliced

2 sage leaves

a small bunch of celery tops (optional – if you happen to have some celery in the fridge already)

300 g frozen peas

20 ml single cream

salt and black pepper

kitchen string

Heat the oil in a saucepan over medium heat. Add the onion and cook gently for 5 minutes, stirring frequently.

Tie together the sage leaves and celery tops, if using, with a piece of kitchen string (for easy removal) and add to the onion along with the peas. Stir, cover and cook for 10 minutes, stirring occasionally.

Uncover, stir through the cream and heat through. Take off the heat and, using a potato masher, gently mash the peas until just crushed – they should retain some texture. Season to taste with salt and pepper and serve immediately.

roast *butternut squash*

Arguably the best-tasting squash and deep gold when roasted, butternut squash is an ideal accompaniment to so many dishes. If you roast it at a high heat, it will brown like a potato, or when cooked more gently, it marries well with fresh herbs.

1 large butternut squash or 2 small ones

2 tablespoons olive oil

75 g unsalted butter

a few sprigs of thyme

2 garlic cloves, sliced

salt and black pepper

Preheat the oven to 190°C (375°F) Gas 5.

Cut the squash in half lengthways and scoop out the seeds and pith with a spoon. Cut each half into 3–4 wedges, according to the size of the squash. There is no need to peel them.

Put the oil and butter in a roasting tin and heat on top of the stove until melted. Add the wedges of butternut squash and baste the pieces, turning them carefully to cover. Push the sprigs of thyme and slices of garlic between the wedges and sprinkle with salt and pepper.

Roast in the preheated oven for 30 minutes, turning the pieces over a couple of times to brown them lightly as they finish cooking.

sweet potato skewers

These potatoes are skewered through the centre, then cut around to free each slice, leaving the skewer in place. This browns the slices individually without letting them fall to pieces. They are really good at picking up flavours from whatever else is in the tin, so bake them with a nut roast or similar.

6 smallish sweet potatoes

3 tablespoons butter, melted

salt and black pepper

6 metal skewers

Preheat the oven to 220°C (425°F) Gas 7.

Peel the sweet potatoes and skewer each one lengthways through the centre. Slice them around the skewer and separate the rounds.

Arrange them around a nut roast (or alone) in a roasting tin, baste generously with the melted butter and season lightly with salt and pepper.

Roast in the preheated oven for 45 minutes or until browned – continue to baste them from time to time to prevent them from drying out.

roast butternut squash

sesame sugar snap peas

1 tablespoon sunflower oil

400 g sugar snap peas

2 teaspoons sesame seeds

2 teaspoons sesame oil

serves
4

Q

These are the perfect accompaniment to a stir-fry or some simple fried tofu.

Heat a wok or frying pan over high heat until hot, then add the sunflower oil. When the oil is hot, add the sugar snap peas. Stir-fry for about 4 minutes, stirring continuously, until tender. Add the sesame seeds and oil and stir-fry for 1 minute more. Serve immediately.

home-made baked beans

1.7 kg tinned beans, such as haricot, cannellini or borlotti, rinsed and drained

3 onions, finely chopped

4 garlic cloves, crushed

2 tablespoons olive oil

1–1½ teaspoons paprika

1½–2 tablespoons molasses or dark muscovado sugar

3 tablespoons tomato purée

4 teaspoons Worcestershire sauce (optional)

500 ml boiling water

salt and black pepper

serves
15!

Ready-prepared baked beans are so cheap to buy that it may seem like madness to make your own but most commercially prepared versions are extremely high in salt and sugar. This may seem like a large quantity to make, but the beans freeze well. To freeze, leave to cool, then transfer to freezerproof containers. Freeze for up to 1 month. Serve the traditional way, on yummy buttered toast, or on a baked sweet potato.

Preheat the oven to 180°C (350°F) Gas 4.

Put the beans in a large casserole dish, add all the remaining ingredients and season lightly with salt and pepper. Mix well.

Cover and cook in the preheated oven for 1–1¼ hours, stirring occasionally, until the sauce is thick and rich in taste and texture. Check the seasoning; add extra Worcestershire sauce, if necessary, and extra molasses or sugar if slightly bitter.

*chilli greens
with garlic crisps*

chilli *greens* with *garlic* crisps

The word 'greens' – used to describe any leafy green – includes spring greens, Swiss chard, pak choi, spinach and more. Many need only brief cooking – steam or stir-fry to retain colour, nutrients and flavour. Remove any tough stalks before cooking.

serves
4

Q

Chop the greens (if using pak choi, cut lengthways into wedges). Heat the olive oil in a large saucepan. Add the garlic, fry until golden and crisp, about 2–3 minutes, then remove and set aside. Add the chilli to the infused oil in the pan and cook for 1 minute. Tip in the greens – they will splutter, so stand back. Add salt and pepper and mix well. Cover and cook, turning occasionally using tongs, until tender: spring greens, about 5 minutes; Swiss chard, pak choi, about 3 minutes; and spinach, about 1–2 minutes.

Transfer to a dish and top with the garlic crisps to serve.

500 g greens (see Introduction, left)

2 tablespoons olive oil

4 garlic cloves, sliced

1 red chilli, deseeded and thinly sliced

salt and black pepper

light bites and sides   **37**

salads

*tabbouleh with chickpeas
and spring salad*

tabbouleh with *chickpeas* and *spring salad*

When buying salad leaves, keep in mind you will need about two large handfuls per person. The fresh ingredients are combined here with bulghur wheat, a nutty grain that is more nutritious than rice or couscous. Simply cover with boiling water to soften and add to your favourite salad ingredients.

Put the bulghur wheat in a heatproof bowl and pour over the boiling water. Stir once, cover tightly with clingfilm and set aside for 8–10 minutes.

Put the lemon juice and olive oil in a small bowl and whisk. Pour over the bulghur wheat and stir well with a fork, fluffing up the bulghur and separating the grains.

Put the bulghur wheat in a large bowl with the parsley, mint, tomatoes, chickpeas and salad leaves. Use your hands to toss everything together. Season well with salt and black pepper.

serves 4

Q

90 g fine bulghur wheat

125 ml boiling water

2 tablespoons lemon juice

60 ml olive oil

a small handful of parsley, freshly chopped

a large handful of mint, freshly chopped

1 small punnet of cherry tomatoes, halved

400-g tin chickpeas, rinsed and drained

120–150 g spring salad mix

salt and black pepper

black bean and *avocado* salad

The combination of colours and textures in this salad is a knockout. It can be made with other pulses, but black beans work particularly well, as they highlight the colours of the other ingredients.

Put the beans in a large salad bowl and add the sweetcorn, red pepper, herbs and olive oil. Stir well and cover until required.

When ready to serve, peel and stone the avocado, then cut into small cubes and put in a small bowl. Add the lemon juice, season with salt and pepper and mix well. Add the avocado to the bean salad and mix well. Taste and add more salt and pepper, if necessary, then serve.

serves 4

Q

2 x 400-g tins black turtle beans, drained

400 g tinned sweetcorn, drained

1 large red pepper, deseeded and diced

a handful of parsley, freshly chopped

a handful of basil, freshly chopped

3 tablespoons olive oil

1 avocado

1 tablespoon lemon juice

salt and black pepper

90 g bulghur wheat

2 spring onions, chopped

1 celery stalk, finely chopped

1 red pepper, deseeded and finely chopped

1 green apple, cored and chopped

Dressing

1 tablespoon grainy mustard

1 tablespoon runny honey

2 tablespoons cider or white wine vinegar

2 tablespoons mayonnaise

a handful of parsley, freshly chopped

black pepper

150 g feta, cubed

1 garlic clove, crushed

2 tablespoons freshly chopped dill

2 tablespoons freshly chopped mint

4 tablespoons olive oil

grated zest of 1 lemon and juice of ½ lemon

1 small, crisp lettuce, chopped

185 g tomatoes, chopped

185 g cucumber, chopped

50 g stoned black olives

1 small red onion, chopped

1 ripe avocado, peeled, stoned and chopped

black pepper

apple and *bulghur wheat* salad

 serves 4–6

Bulghur wheat-based salads such as tabbouleh are quick, easy and substantial. You could also substitute another grain, such as barley, cooked according to the packet instructions.

Put the bulghur wheat in a bowl and cover with cold water. Leave to soak for 30 minutes until tender but not too soft. Drain well and press down hard on the bulghur wheat with the back of a spoon to squeeze out excess water.

Put the bulghur wheat in a salad bowl with the spring onions, celery, red pepper and apple.

To make the dressing, whisk together the mustard, honey, vinegar and mayonnaise in a small bowl and add black pepper to taste. Add this to the bulghur mixture, cover and refrigerate until needed.

Remove the salad from the refrigerator about 30 minutes before serving and bring to room temperature. Stir in the chopped parsley to serve.

lemon and *herb feta* salad

 serves 2

Q

Marinate the cheese for as long as you like – it will keep in the fridge overnight. Keep the tomatoes out of the fridge as they taste much better and sweeter at room temperature; also make sure you choose ripe tomatoes and ripe, ready-to-eat avocado.

Put the feta cubes in a shallow bowl. In another small bowl mix together the garlic, herbs, olive oil, lemon zest and lemon juice. Season the dressing with pepper and pour over the feta. Cover and leave to marinate for a few minutes in a cool place, or in a refrigerator for longer.

Arrange the salad leaves in 2 bowls. Put the tomatoes, cucumber, olives, onion and avocado on the top, then spoon the marinated feta over the salad. Drizzle any remaining dressing over the salad and serve.

*apple and bulghur
wheat salad*

classic italian salad

classic italian salad

If you ask for a mixed salad in Italy, this is what you will get. It's ultra simple but sometimes, on a warm summer's day, that's exactly what you want from a salad.

serves 4

Q

350 g waxy potatoes, peeled

175 g green beans, trimmed

1 tablespoon olive oil, plus extra to serve

50 g stoned black or green olives

1 small crisp lettuce, torn into bite-sized pieces

2 large ripe tomatoes, quartered

3 tablespoons freshly chopped parsley

salt and black pepper

red wine vinegar, to serve

Bring a large saucepan of salted water to the boil, add the potatoes, bring back to the boil and simmer for about 15 minutes or until tender. Add the green beans to the pan 4 minutes before the potatoes are cooked. Drain and cover with cold water to stop the vegetables cooking further. When cold, drain well.

Remove the beans to a bowl, slice the potatoes thickly and add to the beans. Add the olive oil and olives and toss well.

Add the lettuce to the potatoes along with the tomatoes. Toss lightly. Transfer to a serving bowl and sprinkle with parsley. Serve with olive oil, vinegar and salt and pepper so the salad can be dressed at the table.

avocado and *chickpea* salad

This is a fresh and yet instant meal for lazy evenings. Although it's just a salad, it's got eggs, chickpeas and avocados – so it's nice and filling, and ideal with a chunk of bread on the side.

serves 4

Q

2 eggs

250 g baby spinach

400-g tin chickpeas, rinsed and drained

2 ripe avocados, peeled, stoned and chopped

2 teaspoons sweet paprika

Dressing

juice of 1 lemon

3 tablespoons milk

2 tablespoons fromage frais or Greek yoghurt

a bunch of chives, snipped

salt and black pepper

Put the eggs in a small saucepan of water, bring to the boil and cook until hard-boiled, 8–9 minutes. Drain, cool, shell, cut into quarters and set aside.

To make the dressing, put the lemon juice in a bowl with the milk, fromage frais or yoghurt and snipped chives. Season generously with salt and pepper and stir until smooth.

Put the spinach, chickpeas, avocados and eggs in a bowl. Sprinkle with the paprika, then spoon over the dressing.

500 g red cabbage, shredded

3 tablespoons red or white wine vinegar

500 g white cabbage, shredded

125 g carrot, grated

1 large Granny Smith apple, peeled, cored and grated

75 g pumpkin seeds, toasted

salt and black pepper

Dressing

juice of ½ orange

1 tablespoon white wine vinegar

1 teaspoon sugar

1 tablespoon vegetable oil

180 g natural yoghurt

180 g crème fraîche

100 g green beans, trimmed

200 g red or white cabbage, shredded

3 tomatoes, deseeded and sliced

4 spring onions, sliced

50 g roasted peanuts, chopped

Dressing

a handful of coriander

2 red chillies, deseeded

2 garlic cloves, chopped

2 tablespoons light soy sauce

2 tablespoons lime juice

2 tablespoons brown sugar

apple coleslaw

serves 6–8

Plastic tubs of coleslaw are really no match for the real thing and, if you like it but have never made it yourself, you should try this recipe with its light creamy dressing and healthy apple.

Put the red cabbage in a heatproof bowl. Heat the wine vinegar in a small saucepan until just boiling. Stir in a pinch of salt, then pour the mixture over the red cabbage. Toss well. This helps to set the colour.

In a serving bowl, combine the red cabbage, white cabbage, carrot and apple and toss well to combine.

To make the dressing, put the orange juice, vinegar, salt and sugar in a small bowl and use a fork or small whisk to mix. Add the oil, yoghurt and crème fraîche. Mix well and season to taste with pepper.

Pour the dressing over the cabbage mixture and toss well. Taste for seasoning and adjust if necessary – it may need more salt, or more vinegar. Refrigerate for several hours before serving. When ready to serve, sprinkle with toasted pumpkin seeds. This is best eaten on the day it is prepared.

thai coleslaw

serves 4

This hybrid Thai coleslaw is based on the classic 'som tum', usually made from grated green papaya but replaced here with red cabbage. This recipe is a merging of these two classic dishes with a delicious new twist.

To make the dressing, reserve a few coriander leaves, then very finely chop the rest. Very finely chop the chillies and add to the chopped coriander with the garlic, soy sauce, lime juice and sugar and mix well. Set aside.

Blanch the beans in boiling water for 2 minutes. Drain and cover with cold water to stop them cooking further. When cold, drain well. Mix the cabbage, beans, tomatoes and spring onions in a bowl. Pour the dressing on top, toss well to coat and marinate for about 30 minutes. Spoon into bowls, sprinkle with the peanuts and the reserved coriander leaves, then serve.

apple coleslaw

tomato, mozzarella and basil salad

tomato, mozzarella and *basil* salad

serves
4

Q

This classic salad born on the Isle of Capri is hard to beat. It combines three ingredients that work totally in harmony with each other – mozzarella, tomato and basil. Sliced avocado is also a delicious addition (although not traditional). This is the kind of super easy – but quite smart – dish you want to throw together when friends are over for dinner.

2 balls of buffalo mozzarella, 150 g each

2 large ripe tomatoes, roughly the same size as the balls of mozzarella

50 g basil leaves

about 100 ml olive oil

salt and black pepper

Cut the mozzarella and tomatoes into slices about 5 mm thick. Arrange the tomato slices on a large plate and season with salt and pepper. Put 1 slice of mozzarella on each slice of tomato and top with a basil leaf. Tear up the remaining basil and scatter over the top. Drizzle with a generous amount of olive oil just before serving.

This salad must be made at the last moment to prevent the tomatoes from weeping and the mozzarella from drying out. Serve at room temperature, never chilled, as this would kill the flavours.

Variation If using avocado, halve and peel one ripe avocado, remove the stone and slice the flesh. Intersperse the slices of avocado with the tomato and mozzarella.

grated *cucumber, soured cream* and *paprika* salad

This is strictly speaking a salad, but it works well on a baked potato. For meat-eating friends, serve it with cold chicken.

serves 4

Wash the cucumbers in warm soapy water to remove any wax or residues. Rinse and dry well. Grate them on the rough side of a cheese grater – it shouldn't be too fine. Transfer to a sieve or colander set over a plate, sprinkle with salt and mix well. Let drain for 30 minutes.

Rinse the grated cucumber under cold running water, pat dry with a clean tea towel, then transfer to a bowl. Add the onions and vinegar and mix with a fork. Season well with salt and pepper. Spread the cucumber mixture in an even layer on a serving plate.

Season the soured cream with salt, pepper and a pinch of paprika, then spoon it over the top of the cucumber mixture. Sprinkle liberally with the remaining paprika and serve immediately.

2 large cucumbers

a bunch of spring onions, trimmed and very finely shredded or 1 small red onion, very finely chopped

2 teaspoons white wine vinegar

6 tablespoons soured cream

2 teaspoons sweet paprika

salt and black pepper

feta salad with *sugar snap peas*

The heat of the chilli, the cool of the yoghurt and cucumber together with the saltiness of the feta make this refreshing salad just perfect for summer lunches.

serves 4

Q

Blanch the sugar snap peas in boiling water for 30 seconds. Drain and cover with cold water to stop them cooking further. When cold, drain well.

Cook the beans in boiling water for 4 minutes. Drain and cover with cold water to stop them cooking further. When cold, drain well.

To make the dressing, put the yoghurt, olive oil and lemon juice in a small bowl and whisk well.

Put the feta in a large bowl, add the sugar snaps, beans, cucumber and mint. Pour the dressing over the salad, toss well, then serve topped with the chilli, if using.

150 g sugar snap peas

200 g green beans, trimmed

200 g feta, cubed

½ cucumber, deseeded and chopped

a handful of mint, freshly chopped

1 red chilli, deseeded and finely chopped (optional)

salt

Dressing

3 tablespoons Greek yoghurt

1 tablespoon olive oil

1 tablespoon lemon juice

tomato and *bread* salad

2 red peppers, halved and deseeded

2 yellow peppers, halved and deseeded

500 g ripe tomatoes

4 tablespoons red wine vinegar

2 garlic cloves, crushed

125 ml olive oil, plus extra for drizzling

2 tablespoons capers

75 g stoned black olives

1 small or ½ large ciabatta or other white loaf, cubed

a bunch of basil, leaves torn

black pepper

serves 4–6

This is an ingenious Italian peasant salad designed to make good use of very ripe tomatoes and stale (but not mouldy!) bread. The bread drinks up the rich flavours of the tomato and roasted pepper dressing. It's important to use a crusty, firm-crumbed bread so it doesn't revert to a soggy, dough-like state.

Preheat the grill to high.

Put the peppers cut-side down on a baking tray and grill until blistered and charred. Transfer to a plastic bag, seal and leave to cool (the steam will loosen the skin, making it easier to peel). Scrape off and discard the skin, then cut the peppers into strips, reserving any juice.

Halve the tomatoes and scoop out the cores and seeds over a bowl to catch the juice. Purée the cores and seeds in a blender, then press the extra juice through a sieve into the bowl. Discard the pulp and seeds. Cut the tomato halves into strips.

Put the tomato juice, vinegar, garlic and some black pepper in a bowl. Gradually add the olive oil, whisking until blended.

Mix the strips of peppers and tomatoes in a bowl, add the capers, olives, ciabatta and basil and mix. Add the dressing, toss well to coat, then set aside for 1 hour to infuse. Drizzle with olive oil and serve.

*tomato, avocado
and lime salad
with crisp tortillas*

tomato, avocado and *lime* salad with crisp *tortillas*

This salad makes a tasty addition to a Mexican dish. The crisp tortillas are a great idea as they give the dish an extra bite.

serves
6

Q

Put the lime juice in a bowl. Cut the avocados in half, remove the stones and peel. Cut each half into 4 wedges and toss with the lime juice.

Using a small knife, cut the top and bottom off of the lime. Cut away the skin and pith. Carefully slice between each segment and remove the flesh. Combine the lime flesh with the avocados and add the coriander, tomatoes and 4 tablespoons of the oil. Season with salt and pepper and set aside.

Preheat the grill to hot.

In a small bowl, combine the garlic and the remaining oil. Brush the oil and garlic mixture over the tortillas and grill for about 1 minute until brown. Break the toasted tortillas into pieces and scatter over the salad.

juice of 1 lime, plus 1 lime

4 ripe, firm avocados

a handful of coriander, freshly chopped

24 cherry tomatoes, halved

6 tablespoons olive oil

2 garlic cloves, crushed

2 flour tortillas

salt and black pepper

lebanese *halloumi* salad

1 large wholegrain pita
bread, opened out

1 small cucumber, deseeded
and cut into chunks

2 large vine-ripened
tomatoes, deseeded and cut
into chunks

1 small red pepper, deseeded
and sliced

10 stoned black olives, halved

½ small red onion, sliced

3 tablespoons freshly
chopped parsley

3 tablespoons freshly
chopped mint

150 g halloumi (patted dry
with kitchen paper), cubed

Dressing

2 tablespoons olive oil, plus
extra for frying

2 tablespoons lemon juice

½ teaspoon ground cumin
(optional)

salt and black pepper

serves
2

Q

Fresh herbs add colour, flavour and nutritional value to this
Lebanese salad, and although halloumi is not a traditional
ingredient, the cheese adds valuable protein. This is a good
get-ahead lunch – make some for your supper one evening, then
keep the leftovers for lunch the next day. If you do this, only
add the pita just before serving so it remains crisp.

Preheat the grill to medium.

Grill the pita bread until lightly golden and crisp. Leave to cool.

Meanwhile, mix together the oil, lemon juice and cumin, if using, for the
dressing. Season with salt and pepper.

Put the cucumber, tomatoes and red pepper in a serving bowl, then add the
olives, onion, parsley and mint. Pour the dressing over and toss until
combined. Break the crisp pita into pieces and mix into the salad.

Heat a little oil in a frying pan and fry the halloumi until it starts to colour.
Divide the salad between 2 plates, then top with the halloumi.

*garden salad with
garlic toasts*

garden salad with *garlic* toasts

The best thing about this salad is that you can use whatever salad leaves you can find that look ultra crisp and fresh. These are then spruced up with cheat's croutons, chunks of cheese and the best home-made salad cream you can imagine.

serves
4

Q

Preheat the grill to medium.

To make the salad cream, put the salt, sugar, mustard, vinegar and oil in a bowl and whisk to dissolve the salt and sugar. Begin to add the milk, very slowly at first and whisking the whole time. Continue to add all of the milk until you have a dressing the consistency of a thin custard.

Brush a little oil over each side of the bread slices. Lightly grill the bread until golden on both sides and rub the garlic cloves over the toast. Allow the toast to cool and crisp up.

Hard-boil the eggs following the instructions in the Avocado and Chickpea Salad recipe on page 45. Drain, cool, shell, cut into quarters and combine with the remaining ingredients in a large bowl. Roughly break up the pieces of toast and add to the salad with some of the salad cream, then gently toss to combine. Serve immediately.

6 thin slices of bread

3–4 garlic cloves

2 eggs

3 large handfuls of salad, such as Little Gem, butterhead and frisée

3 ripe tomatoes

1 bunch of spring onions

200 g Cheddar

olive oil, for brushing

Salad cream

1 teaspoon salt

1 teaspoon caster sugar

1 tablespoon mild mustard

1 tablespoon white wine vinegar

60 ml olive oil

100 ml milk

warm *potato* salad

This versatile salad can be eaten hot or cold, as a meal in itself or, for meat-eaters, as an accompaniment to grilled chicken.

serves
4

Boil the potatoes in a large saucepan of simmering water for 15–20 minutes until the potatoes are tender when pierced with a fork. Drain and leave to cool slightly. When cool enough to handle, cut them into 2.5-cm cubes and put in a serving bowl.

Hard-boil the eggs following the instructions in the Avocado and Chickpea Salad recipe on page 45. Drain, cool, shell, and chop.

Put the yoghurt, crème fraîche and garlic in a separate bowl and mix. Spoon the mixture over the potatoes, add the cucumber, pepper and eggs and stir carefully. Serve hot or cold.

450 g salad potatoes, such as Pink Fir or Charlotte, unpeeled

2 eggs

1 tablespoon natural yoghurt

1 tablespoon crème fraîche

1 garlic clove, crushed

½ cucumber, finely chopped

1 small red pepper, deseeded and finely chopped

cauliflower and swiss chard salad with chickpeas

65 ml olive oil

1 small head of cauliflower, separated into large florets

1 teaspoon ground cumin

6 large Swiss chard leaves, chopped into 2-cm-wide strips

1 red onion, cut into wedges

2 garlic cloves, chopped

400-g tin chickpeas, rinsed and drained

65 ml tahini (sesame seed paste)

2 tablespoons lemon juice

¼ teaspoon black pepper

salt

This is such a fantastic and unusual warm salad. It's light and slightly spicy, with a Middle-Eastern flavour.

Heat the oil in a frying pan over high heat, add the cauliflower florets and cook for 8–10 minutes, turning often, until they are a dark, golden brown. Add the cumin and cook, stirring, for 1 minute. Add the Swiss chard, onion and garlic to the pan and cook for a further 2–3 minutes. Add the chickpeas and stir. Season to taste with salt.

Combine the tahini, lemon juice and pepper in a small bowl and add a little salt to taste. Whisk to combine. Transfer the vegetables to a bowl and drizzle the dressing over the top to serve.

warm puy lentil salad

100 g cherry tomatoes

300 g Puy lentils or other brown lentils

grated zest and juice of 1 lemon

1 dried bay leaf

2 garlic cloves, chopped

2 red onions, diced

75 g stoned green olives

a handful of parsley, freshly chopped

4 tablespoons olive oil, plus extra for frying

salt and black pepper

100 g Parmesan or mozzarella, to serve (optional)

Really, this is a salad for all seasons. It works wonderfully served warm or cold and is bound to become a regular feature in your cooking repertoire.

Preheat the oven to 130°C (250°F) Gas 1.

Grease a baking tray with olive or vegetable oil. Put the cherry tomatoes on the tray and cook in the preheated oven for 40 minutes.

Meanwhile, put the lentils in a saucepan. Add the lemon zest and juice, bay leaf, garlic and enough water to cover. Stir, bring to the boil, then simmer for about 40 minutes or until the lentils are soft.

Drain the lentils thoroughly and transfer to a large bowl. Add the tomatoes, red onion, olives, parsley, olive oil, salt and pepper. Toss gently, then serve topped with slices of Parmesan or mozzarella, if using.

cauliflower and swiss chard
salad with chickpeas

*warm chickpea salad with
spiced mushrooms*

warm *chickpea* salad with spiced *mushrooms*

This main-course salad was inspired by Middle-Eastern cuisine, where beans, yoghurt and mint are widely used. Make this dish more substantial by serving it with couscous or bulghur wheat.

serves 4

Q

Heat 2 tablespoons of the oil in a frying pan over medium heat. Add the mushrooms, season with salt and cook until softened. Reduce the heat, then add the garlic, chilli and chickpeas. Fry for 2 minutes, then add the cumin and half the lemon juice. Cook until the juices in the pan evaporate, then set aside.

Put the yoghurt in a bowl, then add the chopped mint and the remaining lemon juice and oil. Add salt and pepper and mix until blended. Divide the spinach between 4 plates, add the chickpea and mushroom mixture, then pour the yoghurt dressing over the top and serve.

3 tablespoons olive oil

300 g button mushrooms

2 garlic cloves, chopped

1 red chilli, deseeded and chopped

400-g tin chickpeas, rinsed and drained

2 teaspoons ground cumin

juice of 1 lemon

175 ml Greek or thick natural yoghurt

a large handful of mint, freshly chopped

250 g baby spinach

salt and black pepper

char-grilled *asparagus* and *leaf* salad with *sesame-soy* dressing

Char-grilling is one of the best ways of cooking asparagus spears – it seals in their sweet, earthy flavour. Turn this salad into a main dish by adding boiled eggs.

serves 2–3

Q

Lightly toast the sesame seeds in a dry frying pan, stirring frequently, until golden and popping. Transfer to a bowl and leave to cool.

Wash the asparagus and cut off any tough stalks. Brush with olive oil. Heat a stove-top griddle pan or frying pan until very hot, add the asparagus (in batches, if necessary) and cook, turning occasionally, until bright green, blistered and slightly charred, about 5–7 minutes (depending on thickness).

Put the toasted sesame seeds, soy sauce and balsamic vinegar in a bowl and gradually whisk in the oil until emulsified. To assemble, put the salad leaves on a platter, arrange the asparagus on top, drizzle with the sesame dressing and serve.

2 tablespoons sesame seeds

a bunch of asparagus, about 12 spears

1 tablespoon dark soy sauce

1 tablespoon balsamic vinegar

3 tablespoons olive oil, plus extra for brushing

150 g mixed salad leaves, such as rocket, watercress and spinach

warm *goats' cheese* salad

serves
4

Q

200 g mixed salad leaves

350 g goats' cheese with rind, cut into 4 rounds

2 avocados, peeled, stoned and chopped

100 g shelled pecan nuts, toasted

salt and black pepper

Dressing

1 tablespoon sugar

1 teaspoon tomato purée

2 tablespoons balsamic vinegar

6 tablespoons olive oil

2 ripe tomatoes, deseeded and finely chopped

Nothing beats grilled goats' cheese – warm, slightly caramelized and oozingly good – especially served on a tasty salad.

To make the dressing, put the sugar and 1 tablespoon water into a heavy-based saucepan. Heat gently, whisking constantly until the sugar has dissolved. Transfer the sugar syrup to a bowl and add the tomato purée and balsamic vinegar, whisking rapidly until thoroughly combined. Add the olive oil slowly, whisking constantly until emulsified. Add the tomatoes and mix well. Set aside.

Divide the salad leaves between 4 plates and season to taste with salt and pepper. Heat a large non-stick frying pan over medium-high heat. Add the goats' cheese slices and cook until they start to bubble and brown in places, about 5 minutes.

Arrange the avocados and pecan nuts over the salad leaves. Drizzle the dressing over the top. Lift a slice of goats' cheese onto the centre of each plate. Top with a little more dressing.

thrown-together *olives, tomatoes* and *feta*

serves
4–6

250 g tomatoes, halved

brown sugar, to taste

2 garlic cloves, thinly sliced

200 g stoned green olives

200 g stoned black olives

200 g feta, cubed

2 tablespoons chilli oil (optional)

2 tablespoons olive oil

grated zest of ½ lemon

a handful of basil leaves

salt

This a popular tapas recipe in Spain. Eat it as a snack or as a little salad in itself. The recipe makes a generous amount so keep any leftovers in a covered bowl in the refrigerator to enjoy over several days.

Preheat the oven to 200°C (400°F) Gas 6.

Remove the hard core from the tomatoes by making a V-shaped incision with a sharp knife. Put the tomatoes on a baking tray and sprinkle with salt and brown sugar. Push a slice of garlic into the soft seeds of each tomato, then roast in the preheated oven for 1 hour until quite dry.

Put the tomatoes in a serving bowl, add the olives, feta, chilli oil, if using, olive oil and lemon zest. Toss well, top with the basil, then serve.

warm goats' cheese salad

pasta

*penne with
tomatoes and basil*

penne with *tomatoes* and *basil*

This pasta dish couldn't be simpler, but you do need to leave the garlic, olive oil and basil to infuse the tomatoes for about an hour to become deliciously fragrant. The end result is a fabulous taste of Italy.

serves
4

400 g ripe cherry tomatoes, halved

2 garlic cloves, crushed

100 ml olive oil

a small handful of basil, leaves torn

400 g dried penne

salt and black pepper

Put the tomatoes and garlic in a large bowl. Pour over the olive oil. Season with salt and pepper, add half the basil and leave for an hour or so to infuse. A warmish place is best, or at room temperature, but not the fridge because the cold will stop the oil from absorbing the flavours.

Bring a big saucepan of water to the boil and add a pinch of salt. Drop in the pasta and cook according to the instructions on the packet.

Drain the pasta and add it to the bowl with the infused tomatoes. Toss well so that the oil coats all the pieces and finally stir in the remaining torn basil.

wholemeal spaghetti with *courgettes* and *herbs*

The nutty taste of wholemeal pasta works brilliantly here with the bright flavours of mint, chilli and lemon.

 serves
4

 Q

400 g dried wholemeal spaghetti

65 ml olive oil

6 courgettes, grated

2 red onions, finely chopped

2 garlic cloves, chopped

1 tablespoon lemon juice

½ teaspoon dried chilli flakes

a large handful of mint, freshly chopped

a large handful of parsley, freshly chopped

grated Parmesan, to serve

salt

Bring a large saucepan of water to the boil and add a pinch of salt. Drop in the pasta and cook according to the instructions on the packet.

Meanwhile, heat the olive oil in a large, heavy-based frying pan set over medium heat. Add the courgettes and onions and cook, stirring, for about 10 minutes, until softened and turning golden.

Add the garlic, lemon juice and chilli flakes and cook for 1 minute further. Remove from the heat.

Drain the pasta and add to the pan with the courgette mixture. Add the herbs and toss well to combine. Serve immediately, sprinkled with some grated Parmesan.

farfalle with *courgettes, sultanas* and *pine nuts*

2 tablespoons sultanas

400 g dried farfalle

3 tablespoons olive oil

3 medium courgettes, thinly sliced

3 tablespoons pine nuts

2 garlic cloves, crushed

grated zest of 1 lemon

salt and black pepper

serves 4

This is a lovely vegetarian pasta dish, but it's such a delicious mixture of flavours and textures that everyone seems to love it. Any short pasta shape would work nicely, so if you have a particular favourite, don't be afraid to try it.

Put the sultanas into a little dish and cover them with hot water. Leave them for about 15 minutes, until they are nice and plump.

Bring a large saucepan of water to the boil and add a pinch of salt. Drop in the pasta and cook according to the instructions on the packet.

Heat the olive oil in a large saucepan over medium heat and fry the courgettes for 6–8 minutes, until golden. Add the pine nuts and cook for a further 2–3 minutes, until the pine nuts are golden.

Add the garlic and cook for just 2 minutes; you don't want it to cook so much that it browns, which is when it becomes bitter.

Drain the sultanas and stir them into the mixture together with the lemon zest. Season the mixture to taste with salt and pepper.

Drain the pasta and toss with the courgette and sultana mixture.

pappardelle with *parsley*

400 g dried pappardelle

a bunch of parsley, freshly chopped

1 garlic clove, finely chopped

4 tablespoons olive oil

juice of ½ lemon

salt and black pepper

serves 4

Q

Pappardelle is like flat, wide spaghetti. Because of its extra width, whatever sauce you add, it will cling more easily and give more flavour. This is the kind of recipe you can turn to when your kitchen cupboards are looking horribly bare.

Bring a large saucepan of water to the boil and add a pinch of salt. Drop in the pasta and cook according to the instructions on the packet.

Drain the pasta and return it to the pan, off the heat. Add the parsley, garlic, oil, lemon juice and salt and pepper to taste. Toss well, then serve.

farfalle with courgettes,
sultanas and pine nuts

*spaghetti with butternut
squash, sage and pecorino*

spaghetti with butternut squash, sage and pecorino

This tasty pasta is inspired by the classic Italian dish of pumpkin-filled ravioli with sage butter except this is an inside-out version and therefore much easier to make.

Bring a large saucepan of water to the boil and add a pinch of salt. Drop in the pasta and cook according to the instructions on the packet.

Heat the oil in a frying pan over high heat. Add the squash and cook for 5–6 minutes, turning often, until golden but not breaking up. Add the garlic and sage to the pan and cook for 2–3 minutes. Remove from the heat and leave to sit to allow the flavours to develop.

Drain the pasta well and return to the warm pan with the squash mixture. Add the parsley and half of the Pecorino and season well with salt and pepper. Serve with the remaining cheese sprinkled over the top.

serves
4

Q

400 g dried spaghetti

65 ml olive oil

400 g butternut squash, peeled, deseeded and cut into thin wedges

2 garlic cloves, chopped

10–12 small fresh sage leaves

a handful of parsley, freshly chopped

50 g Pecorino, grated or shaved with a vegetable peeler

salt and black pepper

spaghetti with herbs and garlic

If you like chillies, there is a similar dish to this that includes a couple of chopped chillies or a pinch of chilli flakes with the garlic-infused olive oil. Never be afraid to experiment – that's how we discover new things!

Bring a large saucepan of water to the boil and add a pinch of salt. Drop in the pasta and cook according to the instructions on the packet.

Heat the oil in a frying pan over medium heat. Add the whole garlic cloves to the frying pan and leave to warm and infuse the oil for 3–4 minutes.

Fish the garlic out of the oil with a slotted spoon and discard.

Drain the pasta and toss with the garlic-infused oil, the lemon zest and the herbs. Serve at once with grated Parmesan.

serves
4

Q

400 g dried spaghetti

100 ml olive oil

3 garlic cloves, peeled but left whole

grated zest of 1 lemon

a large handful of mixed fresh herbs (such as chives, parsley and basil), leaves torn

grated Parmesan, to serve

penne with *mozzarella, herbs* and *tomatoes*

serves
4

Q

There's so much flavour packed into this dish that you'll come back to it time and time again when you don't know what to cook for your dinner. Use whichever fresh herbs you already have or can most easily find. Consider buying a jar of capers and keeping it on standby in the fridge for recipes such as this – capers always come in handy, and they are great at pepping up an otherwise bland dish.

400 g dried penne

400-g tin chopped tomatoes

1 small dried red chilli

3–4 garlic cloves, chopped

1 onion, chopped

2 tablespoons tomato purée

leaves from 2 sprigs of oregano, marjoram, basil or rosemary, freshly chopped

1 tablespoon sugar

50 g capers or stoned black olives, rinsed and drained (optional)

150 g mozzarella, thinly sliced

2 tablespoons olive oil

salt and black pepper

Bring a large saucepan of water to the boil and add a pinch of salt. Drop in the pasta and cook according to the instructions on the packet.

Put the tomatoes in a large, shallow saucepan or frying pan. Add the chilli, garlic, onion, tomato purée, oregano (or other herb), sugar and capers or olives. Cook, stirring, over high heat until the sauce is thick and reduced to about half its original volume. Add salt and pepper to taste. Fish out the whole chilli and discard.

Drain the pasta, reserving 3 tablespoons of the cooking liquid, then return the pasta and reserved liquid to the saucepan. Add the sliced mozzarella. Pour the hot sauce over the top and toss and stir until well mixed and the mozzarella is softened and melting. Drizzle with the olive oil and serve.

penne with mozzarella, herbs and tomatoes

spaghetti with *peas* and *mint*

Try to use little French petits pois for this pasta dish instead of larger garden peas. They have a sweeter flavour and a satisfying pop when you bite into them. Buy them frozen and keep a stash in the freezer.

serves
2–4

Q

300 g spaghetti

80 g peas (fresh or frozen)

125 ml crème fraîche

a handful of mint, freshly chopped

salt and black pepper

Bring a large saucepan of water to the boil and add a pinch of salt. Drop in the pasta and cook according to the instructions on the packet. About 2 minutes before the pasta is cooked add the peas to the boiling water.

Drain the pasta and peas and return them to the warm pan with the crème fraîche and mint. Gently toss to combine and coat the pasta in the softened crème fraîche. Season well with salt and pepper and serve.

fusilli with tomatoey sauce

fusilli with tomatoey sauce

This sauce is more substantial and has a stronger flavour than basic tomato sauce – it contains celery, carrot and onion, finely chopped so that they blend in with the tomatoes. Simmer for an hour to allow the sauce time to thicken and become richer.

serves 4–6

Heat the butter and olive oil in a heavy-based saucepan over high heat. When it starts to bubble, add the celery, carrot, onion, herbs and tomatoes. Stir quickly in the hot fat for a few minutes, then lower the heat, cover and simmer for 1 hour. Stir from time to time, adding a little water as the tomatoes reduce.

Bring a large saucepan of water to the boil and add a pinch of salt. Drop in the pasta and cook according to the instructions on the packet.

Push the sauce though a sieve. Add salt and pepper to taste. Toss the sauce through the warm pasta, then sprinkle with Parmesan.

25 g butter

2 tablespoons olive oil, plus extra to serve

1 small celery stalk, finely chopped

1 small carrot, finely chopped

1 small onion, finely chopped

a small handful of basil or other herbs, freshly chopped

1 kg tomatoes, deseeded and chopped

500 g dried fusilli

salt and black pepper

grated Parmesan, to serve

pasta with purple sprouting broccoli, chilli and pine nuts

Purple sprouting broccoli is sweeter and more tender than regular broccoli. It's a little dearer but worth it for this dish.

serves 4

Q

Bring a large saucepan of water to the boil and add a pinch of salt. Drop in the pasta and cook according to the instructions on the packet. Drain and return to the warm pan.

Bring another saucepan of water to the boil and add a pinch of salt. Cook the broccoli florets for 2 minutes and drain well.

Heat the butter and oil in a frying pan over medium heat. When it starts to bubble, add the chillies, garlic and pine nuts and cook for 3–4 minutes, stirring often, until the garlic has softened and the pine nuts are starting to turn golden. Add the broccoli and stir to coat in the other ingredients. Add the broccoli mixture to the pasta with the Parmesan and stir well.

400 g dried orecchiette, or other small pasta shapes

400 g purple sprouting broccoli, chopped

50 g butter

2 tablespoons olive oil

2 small red chillies, deseeded and finely chopped

2 garlic cloves, sliced

40 g pine nuts

50 g Parmesan, grated

spaghetti with tomatoes and aubergines

400 g dried spaghetti or penne

1 aubergine, about 350 g, cubed

500 g cherry tomatoes, halved and deseeded

125 ml olive oil

125 ml passata (sieved tomatoes) or tomato juice

2 garlic cloves, chopped

a large handful of basil, leaves torn, to serve

salt and black pepper

serves
4

No long simmering needed for this pasta sauce: the tiny tomato halves are oven-roasted and the cubes of aubergine salted, then sautéed, to intensify the tastes. Use whatever sturdy dry pasta is available: spaghetti, penne and rigatoni all taste excellent in this context. The sauce is relatively dry and relatively minimal. It is deliberate – it works!

Preheat the oven to 230°C (450°F) Gas 8.

Bring a large saucepan of salted water to the boil, ready to add the pasta when the vegetables are half cooked.

Put the aubergine cubes in a non-metallic bowl, then add 1 teaspoon salt and set aside while you cook the tomatoes.

Pack the tomatoes, cut sides up, on a baking tray, sprinkle with salt and drizzle with 2 tablespoons of the oil. Roast in the preheated oven for 10 minutes or until wilted and aromatic.

Cook the pasta according to the instructions on the packet.

Drain the aubergine and pat dry with kitchen paper. Heat 4 tablespoons of the olive oil in a non-stick frying pan. Add the aubergine and cook, stirring, over high heat until frizzled and soft, about 8 minutes. Add the roasted tomato halves, passata or juice, garlic and black pepper. Cook, stirring, for 2–3 minutes, then stir through most of the basil.

Drain the pasta and return to the saucepan. Toss in the remaining olive oil. Divide between bowls and spoon over the sauce. Garnish with the remaining basil leaves.

rigatoni with roasted vegetables

rigatoni with roasted vegetables

When choosing peppers, aubergines, tomatoes and the like, squeeze them lightly to ensure the flesh is firm. Don't worry if they're funny shapes, it's more important that they are fresh.

serves 4

- 400 g dried rigatoni or penne
- 1 small aubergine, about 100 g
- 1 red pepper, deseeded
- 1 yellow pepper, deseeded
- 100 g courgettes
- 100 g leeks
- 1½ tablespoons freshly chopped rosemary leaves
- 2 garlic cloves, crushed
- 2 tablespoons olive oil
- 1–2 tablespoons capers, rinsed and drained
- 100 g cherry tomatoes
- grated Parmesan, to serve

Preheat the oven to 200°C (400°F) Gas 6.

Bring a large saucepan of water to the boil and add a pinch of salt. Drop in the pasta and cook according to the instructions on the packet.

Cut the aubergine, peppers, courgettes and leeks into bite-sized pieces, about 2 cm square, and arrange in a single layer in a roasting tin. Add the rosemary, garlic and olive oil and mix well. Cover with aluminium foil and roast in the preheated oven for 20–30 minutes until tender.

Discard the foil, add the capers and tomatoes, stir and roast for 10 minutes.

Drain the pasta and stir into the roasted vegetables. Serve with Parmesan.

farfalle with roasted squash, feta and sage

Roasting the squash and onion first adds a slightly smoky flavour to this pasta sauce. You can use either butternut squash or pumpkin – in either case you will need a 750-g vegetable to yield 500 g flesh.

serves 4

- 500 g butternut squash or pumpkin flesh, diced
- 1 small red onion, thinly sliced
- 1 tablespoon freshly chopped sage
- 5 tablespoons olive oil
- 400 g dried farfalle
- 4 garlic cloves, finely chopped
- a pinch of dried chilli flakes
- 50 g pine nuts
- 200 g feta, diced
- salt and black pepper

Preheat the oven to 220°C (425°F) Gas 7.

Put the squash, onion, sage, 1 tablespoon of the olive oil and some seasoning in a roasting tin, toss well and roast in the preheated oven for 30 minutes, or until the vegetables are golden and cooked through.

Bring a large saucepan of water to the boil and add a pinch of salt. Drop in the pasta and cook according to the instructions on the packet.

Heat the remaining olive oil in a large frying pan and gently fry the garlic, chilli flakes and a little salt and pepper for 2–3 minutes until soft. Add the pine nuts and stir-fry for 2–3 minutes until lightly browned. Add the roasted squash, onions, sage and the feta. Drain the pasta, add to the pan and stir.

big pasta shells stuffed with herbs and ricotta

400 g dried conchiglioni rigati

3 tomatoes, deseeded and chopped

500 g ricotta

2 tablespoons freshly chopped herbs, such as chives, parsley and basil

3 tablespoons olive oil

3 tablespoons grated Parmesan

 serves **4**

 Q

This is ingenious really — a cheat's version of stuffed pasta which requires no time and no skill but still tastes scrumptious.

Preheat the oven to 180°C (350°F) Gas 4.

Bring a large saucepan of water to the boil and add a pinch of salt. Drop in the pasta and cook according to the instructions on the packet. Drain well.

Put the tomatoes in a bowl and stir in the ricotta and mixed herbs. Place a teaspoonful of the mixture into each of the pasta shells and lay them snugly in a baking dish.

Drizzle over the olive oil and scatter over the Parmesan. Bake in the preheated oven for 10 minutes, until hot.

linguine with ricotta, cinnamon and walnuts

500 g dried linguine or rigatoni

250 g ricotta

75 g unsalted butter, softened

1 teaspoon icing sugar

1 teaspoon cinnamon or mixed spice

5 tablespoons chopped walnuts

salt and black pepper

grated Parmesan, to serve

 serves **4–6**

 Q

This is an ideal vegetarian meal — it is more a dressing than a sauce, because there is no cooking. It's so straightforward, it can be prepared in the time it takes to cook the pasta.

Bring a large saucepan of water to the boil and add a pinch of salt. Drop in the pasta and cook according to the instructions on the packet. Drain well, reserving 100 ml of the pasta cooking water.

Put the ricotta, butter, icing sugar and cinnamon in a bowl and beat with a wooden spoon until smooth and creamy. Add salt and pepper to taste and stir in half the reserved pasta water.

Add the ricotta mixture to the drained pasta, with the remaining pasta water if necessary, then stir in the chopped walnuts. Mix well until coated. Serve with grated Parmesan.

*big pasta shells stuffed
with herbs and ricotta*

pasta with basic *cream, butter* and *parmesan* sauce

This sauce provides the base for a variety of other sauces. Stir in some vegetables as a feast for unexpected guests. Add herbs, nuts or cheese to make a delicious sauce for stuffed pasta.

250 ml single cream

25 g unsalted butter

3 tablespoons grated Parmesan, plus extra to serve

250 g dried pasta or fresh, stuffed pasta

3 tablespoons freshly chopped herbs, such as parsley, coriander or basil

grated zest of ½ lemon (optional)

lots of black pepper

Put the cream and butter in a saucepan over low heat. Bring to simmering point, shaking the pan from time to time. Simmer for a few minutes or until the sauce starts to thicken. Add the Parmesan and pepper and stir.

Bring a large saucepan of water to the boil and add a pinch of salt. Drop in the pasta and cook according to the instructions on the packet. Drain well, reserving 100 ml of the pasta cooking water.

Stir the sauce and half of the reserved pasta water into the pasta. Mix until well coated. Add extra pasta water if necessary and stir again. Serve sprinkled with extra Parmesan, chopped herbs and lemon zest, if using.

chilli pasta bake

Fettuccine and tagliatelle take very little time to cook, which makes them the perfect ingredient for a quick evening meal.

250 g dried fettuccine or tagliatelle

2 courgettes, chopped

2 leeks, chopped

2 garlic cloves, crushed

1–2 red chillies, deseeded and finely chopped

1 tablespoon freshly chopped oregano

1 tablespoon freshly chopped parsley

600 ml passata (sieved tomatoes)

3 tablespoons crème fraîche

2 tablespoons grated Parmesan

salt and black pepper

Preheat the oven to 190°C (375°F) Gas 5.

Bring a large saucepan of water to the boil and add a pinch of salt. Drop in the pasta and cook according to the instructions on the packet.

Heat a large non-stick saucepan over medium heat, add the courgettes, leeks and garlic and dry fry for 2–3 minutes. Add the chillies, herbs, passata and crème fraîche. Drain the pasta and add to the chilli sauce. Season to taste with salt and pepper and stir well. Transfer to an ovenproof dish and sprinkle with the grated Parmesan.

Bake in the preheated oven for 30–35 minutes, until golden brown and bubbling. Serve immediately.

*pasta with quick
tomato sauce*

pasta with quick *tomato* sauce

This classic tomato sauce is made simply with tomatoes, olive oil, garlic and the flavouring of your choice.

serves
4–6

Put the tomatoes, oil and garlic in a heavy-based saucepan. Add your choice of flavouring. Cover and simmer over low heat for 30 minutes, or until thickened. Stir from time to time to stop the sauce sticking to the bottom of the pan. Add a little of the reserved tomato juice whenever necessary to keep the sauce moist.

Bring a large saucepan of water to the boil and add a pinch of salt. Drop in the pasta and cook according to the instructions on the packet. Drain well.

Discard the garlic and chilli or cinnamon stick. Mash the sauce with a potato masher. Taste and adjust the seasoning with salt and pepper. Pour the sauce over the pasta, sprinkle with the Parmesan and stir well.

1 kg tinned chopped tomatoes, drained (reserve the juice)

5 tablespoons olive oil

4 garlic cloves

your choice of: 1 small piece of fresh chilli, ½ cinnamon stick, ½ teaspoon dried oregano, or a handful of freshly chopped herbs

500 g dried pasta or fresh, stuffed pasta

3 tablespoons grated Parmesan

salt and black pepper

extra-crispy *macaroni cheese*

The best bit about macaroni and cheese, as we all know, is the crispy topping, so how fantastic would it be to have crispy bits all the way through. Try it and see!

serves 2–3

Preheat the oven to 170°C (325°F) Gas 3.

Sprinkle 50 g of the Cheddar in an even layer over a baking tray. Bake in the preheated oven for 8–10 minutes until bubbling and beginning to brown. Remove from the oven, leave to cool, then break into pieces and set aside.

Put the butter in a medium non-stick saucepan and melt gently. Stir in the flour and cook for a few seconds, then take the pan off the heat and add the milk little by little, stirring before you add the next amount. Put the pan back on the hob, increase the heat slightly, then bring the sauce gradually to the boil, stirring continuously. Turn the heat right down again and let the sauce simmer for 5 minutes, stirring it occasionally.

Bring a large saucepan of water to the boil and add a pinch of salt. Drop in the pasta and cook according to the instructions on the packet.

Meanwhile, preheat the grill.

Just before the pasta is ready, stir half the remaining Cheddar into the sauce, add the mustard and Worcestershire sauce, and season to taste. Add a little more milk if it looks too thick.

Drain the pasta thoroughly and tip into the prepared ovenproof dish. Scatter the crispy cheese pieces over the pasta and mix together. Pour in the cheese sauce, then sprinkle over the remaining Cheddar. Place the dish under the hot grill for about 5 minutes until the top is brown and crispy.

125–150 g strong Cheddar, coarsely grated

25 g butter

25 g plain flour

300 ml whole milk

175 g rigatoni or penne

½ teaspoon mustard

a few drops of Worcestershire sauce

salt and black pepper

a shallow ovenproof dish, lightly buttered

50 g butter

1 medium/large leek, trimmed and thinly sliced

40 g plain flour

600 ml semi-skimmed milk

a head of broccoli divided into small florets (about 300 g florets)

350 g dried penne (plain or wholemeal)

2 handfuls of chard or spinach leaves

150 g mature Gruyère

3 heaped tablespoons grated Parmesan

salt, black pepper and grated nutmeg

4 individual ovenproof dishes, lightly buttered

mac 'n' greens

serves 4

This is a healthy twist on macaroni cheese if you feel that you've had too much indulgent food recently. You can also use wholemeal pasta if you want to make this recipe even more nutritionally balanced.

Put the butter in a medium non-stick saucepan and melt gently. Add the leeks, stir and cook for 1 minute, then stir in the flour and cook for a few seconds. Take the pan off the heat and gradually add the milk, stirring continuously. Put the pan back on the hob, increase the heat slightly, then bring the milk gradually up to simmering point. Turn the heat right down again and leave the sauce over very low heat.

Fill a large saucepan with boiling water from the kettle, bring back to the boil, add salt, then add the broccoli and blanch for a couple of minutes. Transfer the broccoli to a sieve with a slotted spoon and rinse with cold water. Tip the pasta into the same water in the pan and cook according to the instructions on the packet.

Wash and remove the stalk and central rib from the chard or spinach (unless using baby leaves). Just before the pasta is ready, stir half the Gruyère and the Parmesan into the sauce and check the seasoning, adding salt, pepper, nutmeg and more Parmesan, if necessary. Add the broccoli and chard or spinach, stir, and set aside for 3–4 minutes.

Meanwhile, preheat the grill.

Drain the pasta and divide between the prepared dishes. Pour over the sauce and vegetables and mix gently, then sprinkle over the remaining Gruyère. Place the dishes on a baking tray and grill for 5 minutes until the cheese is brown and bubbling.

light mains

bean and vegetable soup

bean and *vegetable* soup

serves 6

This is a little like minestrone and it's packed with vegetables. The vegetables are lightly steamed, not fried, before cooking in the stock, making it a particularly good option when you are on a healthy eating drive. It's delicious with a large chunk of wholemeal bread.

In a large saucepan, soften the onion and garlic in 4 tablespoons of the stock for 5 minutes, with the lid on. Stir in the carrots, mushrooms and courgettes, season and cook for 2 minutes. Stir in the passata and the remaining stock and bring to a simmer, then cover and cook for 10 minutes.

Mix in the beans and cabbage, re-cover the pan and simmer for a further 10 minutes. Adjust the seasoning and stir in the basil just before serving.

1 onion, chopped

2 garlic cloves, crushed

1.2 litres vegetable stock

2 carrots, diced

150 g mushrooms, chopped

2 courgettes, diced

700 ml passata (sieved tomatoes)

400-g tin cannellini beans, drained and rinsed

150 g green cabbage, shredded

3 tablespoons freshly chopped basil

salt and black pepper

white bean soup with *olive* gremolata

serves 6

You can make this soup with any tinned white beans, such as haricot, cannellini or butter beans. The tasty olive gremolata that you spoon on top makes the soup a bit more special.

Heat the oil in a large saucepan and fry the onion, garlic and sage for 5 minutes until golden. Add the potatoes and beans, stir well, then add the stock, bay leaf, and some salt and pepper.

Bring to the boil, cover and simmer gently for 20 minutes until the potatoes are tender. If you like, you can transfer half the soup to a blender or food processor, or use a handheld blender, and blend until smooth, or you can mash half of it with a potato masher. Return to the pan, adjust the seasoning and heat through.

Meanwhile, to make the olive gremolata, finely chop the olives and mix with lemon zest and parsley. Serve the soup in bowls topped with the gremolata.

4 tablespoons olive oil

1 large onion, chopped

2 garlic cloves, crushed

1 teaspoon dried sage

500 g baking potatoes, cubed

2 x 400-g tins white beans, such as haricot, cannellini or butter, rinsed and drained

1 litre vegetable stock

1 dried bay leaf

salt and black pepper

Olive gremolata

175 g stoned black olives

grated zest of 1 lemon

2 tablespoons freshly chopped parsley

roasted *vegetable* soup

700 g ripe plum tomatoes, halved

175 g red onions, finely chopped

150 g carrots, finely chopped

1 small red chilli

2 garlic cloves, peeled but left whole

a few thyme or rosemary sprigs

2 tablespoons olive oil

350 ml passata (sieved tomatoes)

½ teaspoon sugar

a squeeze of lime juice

salt and black pepper

a handful of coriander, freshly chopped

 serves 2

Once everything is peeled and chopped, this rustic chunky soup is surprisingly simple to make. The vegetables are roasted in the oven, which makes their flavour sweet but intense.

Preheat the oven to 200°C (400°F) Gas 6.

Put the tomatoes, onions and carrots in a roasting tin. Add the chilli, garlic, thyme or rosemary sprigs and olive oil and toss until the vegetables are well coated. Roast in the preheated oven for about 25 minutes, turning the vegetables occasionally using a large spoon.

Remove from the oven and discard the chilli. Blend the roasted vegetables, garlic and herbs with the passata in a blender or food processor, or using a handheld blender. Add the sugar, lime juice and 150 ml water, and season well with salt and pepper.

Pour the mixture into a large saucepan and gently heat through. Add the chopped coriander just before serving.

creamy *pea* soup

3 tablespoons olive oil

1 small onion, chopped

1 garlic clove, crushed

1 small potato, about 100 g, chopped

700 g peas (fresh or frozen)

1 litre vegetable stock

3 tablespoons double cream

salt and black pepper

 serves 4

 Q

This is creamy and dreamy and you can make it with frozen peas, so it's quick as well as delicious!

Heat the olive oil in a large saucepan, then add the onion, garlic and potato. Cook over gentle heat for about 8–10 minutes, stirring quite often, until the onion is shiny and the potatoes are starting to soften.

Pour in the peas and the stock. Leave the soup to simmer for about 20 minutes, until the potato is very soft – the potatoes should be easily squashed when you press them with a wooden spoon.

Blend the soup in a blender or food processor, or using a handheld blender. Stir in the cream and season to taste with a little salt and pepper.

roasted vegetable soup

tomato and red lentil soup

serves 4

1 tablespoon olive oil

1 red onion, finely chopped

1 carrot, finely chopped

1 celery stalk, finely chopped

1 garlic clove, crushed

400-g tin chopped tomatoes

1 tablespoon tomato purée

50 g split red lentils

400 ml vegetable stock

a big pinch of salt

a big pinch of black pepper

a big pinch of sugar

2 tablespoons cream, to serve

This tomato soup is thickened with split red lentils and is packed with delicious ingredients. Adding a couple of tablespoons of cream at the end makes it that little bit more luxurious – you can use any cream you like.

Heat the oil in a large saucepan over low heat. Put the onion, carrot, celery and garlic into the pan. Stir gently with a wooden spoon, then cover the pan with a lid and leave to cook very slowly for 5 minutes. Add the tomatoes, tomato purée, red lentils, stock, salt, pepper and sugar. Stir well, then turn up the heat so the mixture comes to the boil.

When the soup has boiled, cover the pan with the lid, then turn down the heat. Simmer for 30 minutes, stirring occasionally.

At the end of the cooking time, take off the lid, turn off the heat and leave the soup to cool for 5 minutes.

Blend the soup in a blender or food processor, or using a handheld blender. Taste – add more salt, pepper or sugar as needed – then carefully warm up the soup over low heat. Stir in the cream and serve.

poached mushrooms with egg noodles

serves 4

4 portobello mushrooms

1 leek, trimmed and chopped

4 shallots

1 dried bay leaf

200 g dried egg noodles

2 courgettes, chopped

100 g baby sweetcorn, trimmed

100 g flat beans, sliced

100 g spinach, chopped

1 tablespoon soy sauce

salt and black pepper

The purity and natural flavours of this noodle dish will make you feel very healthy! Try using tofu instead of mushrooms.

Put the mushrooms into a large saucepan and add the leeks, shallots, bay leaf, salt and pepper. Add water to cover and heat until simmering. Cover with a lid and cook for 20 minutes.

Add the noodles, adding extra water to cover if necessary. Add the courgettes, sweetcorn, beans, spinach and soy sauce. Simmer for a further 4 minutes, until the noodles and all the vegetables are cooked. Serve in bowls with a ladle of the cooking juices.

tomato and red lentil soup

french onion soup

french *onion* soup

This is a popular favourite with lots of people, and is filling enough to be a meal in itself.

serves
4–6

Put the butter and oil in a large saucepan and heat until the butter melts. Add the onions and salt and stir well. Cook over low heat for 20–30 minutes or until the onions are golden brown. Sprinkle the flour over the onions and stir for 2–3 minutes until there is no sign of white specks of flour. Pour a ladle of the stock onto the onions. Stir well, add the remaining stock and simmer, part-covered, for another 20–30 minutes. Add salt and pepper to taste.

Meanwhile, preheat the oven to 170°C (325°F) Gas 3.

To make the croutons, put the bread on a baking tray and toast in the preheated oven for 15 minutes. Brush with the olive oil and rub with the cut garlic clove. Return to the oven for 15 minutes or until the bread is quite dry.

Ladle the soup into heatproof bowls. Put the slices of toast on top and pile the cheese over them. Dot with more butter and cook in the hot oven for about 15 minutes until the cheese has melted.

50 g unsalted butter, plus extra to finish

1 tablespoon olive oil

1 kg onions, thinly sliced

1 teaspoon salt

50 g plain flour

1 litre hot vegetable stock

salt and black pepper

Croutons

8–12 thick slices of bread (about 2 cm thick)

1 tablespoon olive oil

1 large garlic clove, halved

125 g Gruyère, grated

light mains   **93**

indian omelette

indian omelette

Serve this hot or cold, cut into wedges, with chutney or a raita on the side. Choose a raita of your choice from page 20.

Break the eggs into a bowl, add the yoghurt and whisk briefly with a fork, just enough to mix the yolks and whites. Stir in the cumin, coriander, garlic and some salt and pepper.

Heat 1 tablespoon of the oil in a small frying pan. Add the onion, chilli and ginger and fry over medium-high heat for 2–3 minutes, then add the tomatoes and cook for 1–2 minutes. Using a slotted spoon, transfer to the egg mixture and stir gently.

Add the remaining oil to the pan and swirl it around to coat the bottom and sides. Pour the egg mixture into the pan, reduce the heat to low and cook for about 5–6 minutes, or until the underside is golden and the top almost set.

Slide under a preheated grill to finish cooking or put a plate over the top of the pan and invert so the omelette falls onto the plate. Slide back into the pan and cook for 1–2 minutes. Cut into wedges and serve with raita.

serves 2–3

Q

4 large eggs

2 tablespoons natural yoghurt

1 teaspoon ground cumin

2 tablespoons freshly chopped coriander

1 garlic clove, crushed

2 tablespoons sunflower oil

1 onion, finely chopped

1 small red chilli, deseeded and chopped

3 cm fresh ginger, peeled and grated

2 tomatoes, finely chopped

salt and black pepper

omelette with *chives* and *cheese*

A perfectly crumpled, soft omelette oozing with cheese is bliss – perfect for one, when you need something fast and delicious.

Break the eggs into a bowl, add half the chives and some salt and pepper and whisk briefly with a fork.

Heat a small frying pan over high heat until really hot. Add the butter, wait for it to sizzle, then pour in the eggs. Leave them to become nicely golden on the outside – no more than 45 seconds – drawing the cooked edges into the centre. Tilt the pan so the uncooked egg runs into the edges. When the omelette is evenly set, except for a little unset egg, it is done.

Remove the pan from the heat and add the Gruyère or Cheddar and cream in the centre of the omelette. Fold 2 edges of the omelette over, then tilt the pan so you can slide it out and upturn it onto a plate, folded side down. Sprinkle some pepper over the top and finish with the remaining chives.

serves 1

Q

3 eggs

2 tablespoons snipped chives

1 tablespoon butter

25 g Gruyère or Cheddar, grated

1 tablespoon double cream

salt and black pepper

cauliflower and caperberries on halloumi

3 tablespoons olive oil

150 g cauliflower, broken into small florets

1 garlic clove, chopped

25 g caperberries, large ones halved, or capers, drained and rinsed

50 g stoned green olives, sliced

1 tablespoon freshly chopped parsley

2 teaspoons lemon juice

150 g halloumi, cut into ½-cm-thick slices

salt and black pepper

serves 2–3

Q

If you don't fancy halloumi but like the sound of the flavours in this recipe, the cauliflower mixture could also be served as a topping on thick toast.

Heat 2 tablespoons of the olive oil in a frying pan and cook the cauliflower for 8–10 minutes over high heat, stirring often until it browns evenly and starts to crisp up. Add the garlic, caperberries, olives, parsley and lemon juice and cook for 2 minutes, stirring constantly. Season to taste and leave in the pan to keep warm.

Heat the remaining olive oil in a non-stick frying pan set over high heat. Cook the halloumi slices for 1 minute on each side, until golden brown. Transfer the halloumi to plates and spoon the warm cauliflower mixture over each one.

tofu and vegetable wraps

170 g firm tofu

2 large soft tortillas

1 carrot, grated

½ red pepper, deseeded and cut into thin strips

a handful of rocket leaves

salt and black pepper

olive oil, for brushing

Marinade

2 tablespoons soy sauce

1 tablespoon clear honey

1 tablespoon sweet chilli sauce

2 tablespoons tomato ketchup

serves 2

You will need to marinate the tofu for these wraps for an hour so that they soak up all the sweet, spicy flavours.

Pat the tofu dry with kitchen paper and cut it into 4 thick strips. Mix together the ingredients for the marinade in a shallow dish. Add the tofu and spoon the marinade over until well covered. Cover and marinate for 1 hour.

Lightly brush a griddle pan or frying pan with olive oil and heat until hot. Arrange the tofu in the pan and char-grill for 3 minutes each side until golden and it bears the marks of the griddle.

Warm the tortillas – either wrap in foil and warm in the oven or warm in a dry frying pan. Put 2 pieces of tofu down the centre of each tortilla and spoon over any remaining marinade. Divide the carrot, red pepper and rocket between the tortillas, season to taste, then fold in the ends and sides of each tortilla to make a parcel. Cut in half horizontally before serving.

cauliflower and caperberries on halloumi

baked *mushrooms*

Baked mushrooms often come swimming in oil in order to bring out their flavour. This can leave you feeling overloaded before you even get to the end of the meal! This recipe, however, uses garlic, chillies and chives to give lots of flavour, so the fat content can remain low.

serves
4

250 g medium chestnut or portobello mushrooms, wiped

2–4 teaspoons olive oil

1 celery stalk, finely chopped

1–2 large garlic cloves, crushed

1 green chilli, deseeded and finely chopped

50 g breadcrumbs (preferably fresh)

1 tomato, deseeded and chopped

2 tablespoons snipped chives

salt and black pepper

Preheat the oven to 180°C (350°F) Gas 4.

Choose 4 portobello or 8 chestnut mushrooms and remove the stalks. Put the caps stem-side up in an ovenproof dish. Finely chop the remaining mushrooms and all the stalks.

Heat a non-stick frying pan and add 2 teaspoons of the oil. Add the chopped mushrooms, celery, garlic and chilli and fry, stirring frequently, until soft. Leave to cool slightly, then transfer to a bowl.

Add the breadcrumbs, tomato and chives to the bowl, then season to taste with salt and pepper. Mix well, adding a little oil to moisten, if necessary. Fill the mushrooms with the breadcrumb mixture. Pour about 4 tablespoons of water into the dish, then cook in the preheated oven for 12–15 minutes, until the mushrooms are soft and the topping is crisp. Remove from the oven and serve immediately.

Variation For a really quick version (and if you have a blender or food processor), prepare the mushrooms as above. Put the remaining mushrooms with 2 garlic cloves, 50 g wholegrain bread, 6 spring onions, 50 g dried apricots, 25 g shelled pecans and 2 tablespoons coriander leaves in the blender or food processor. Add salt and pepper, to taste. Blend, adding a little lemon juice if necessary, to give a moist stuffing. Fill the mushrooms with this mixture and cook as above.

cottage cheese pancakes with *sweet chilli mushrooms*

175 g self-raising flour

2 large eggs

200 ml milk

125 g cottage cheese

a large pinch of salt

sunflower oil, for frying

Sweet chilli mushrooms

2 large flat mushrooms, sliced

2–3 tablespoons sweet chilli sauce

serves 2

The batter here makes about 15 pancakes – obviously too many for two people, but the remainder can be chilled or frozen for future use. This is the kind of versatile dish that you can enjoy at any time of day – it's especially good for a hearty breakfast.

Put the flour, eggs, milk, cottage cheese and salt in a blender or food processor and blend to a smooth batter. Set the batter aside for 30 minutes to rest.

Lightly oil a large non-stick frying pan and pour a little (about 30 ml) of the batter into the pan to form a round pancake – you will probably be able to cook 3 pancakes at a time. Cook the pancakes for 1½–2 minutes per side until golden. Keep the pancakes you've already made warm while you make the rest.

When all the batter is used, wipe the pan clean, then add 1 tablespoon oil. Fry the mushrooms for about 5 minutes until tender, then remove from the heat and stir in the sweet chilli sauce and 1 tablespoon water.

To serve, put 3 pancakes on each plate and top with the mushrooms. Spoon over any sauce left in the pan.

Variation To make cottage cheese and corn pancakes, stir 140 g tinned, drained sweetcorn into the batter mixture after it has rested. The sweetcorn pancakes are delicious with sliced avocado, or if you're feeding meat-eaters, with grilled bacon and a drizzle of maple syrup.

*raw tomato and herb sauce
on grilled polenta*

raw *tomato* and *herb* sauce on grilled *polenta*

This raw sauce is so versatile. Spoon it onto this great polenta base, or use it as a chunky topping for many dishes, like pasta.

serves
4

Cook the polenta according to the instructions on the packet, adding a little salt and pepper to the mixture. Pour onto the baking tray and form into a mound. Alternatively, pour into the cake tin. Leave to set for at least 1 hour, then cut into 4 slices. If the cooled polenta is too thick, slice it in half horizontally, then cut into slices.

To make the raw tomato and herb sauce, put the tomatoes, spring onions, herbs, salt and pepper into a bowl. Pour over the olive oil and stir gently. Set aside for about 30 minutes so the flavours mingle.

Heat a griddle pan or frying pan until very hot. Working in batches, brush the polenta pieces with olive oil and cook for a few minutes on each side until golden and barred with grill marks. Remove from the pan and keep warm in a low oven while you cook the rest. Put the polenta onto plates and spoon the sauce over the top to serve.

175 g instant polenta

Raw tomato and herb sauce

500 g ripe tomatoes, deseeded and finely chopped

2 spring onions, finely chopped

1 tablespoon freshly chopped parsley

1 tablespoon freshly chopped thyme

4 tablespoons olive oil, plus extra for brushing

salt and black pepper

a baking tray or round cake tin, 20 cm in diameter, oiled

asparagus with *parmesan* and chopped *eggs*

Asparagus and Parmesan are pricey, so this is best kept for a special treat. Try to shave the Parmesan with a vegetable peeler because you'll getter bigger, nicer chunks than if you grate it.

serves
4

Q

Hard-boil the eggs following the instructions in the Avocado and Chickpea Salad recipe on page 45. Drain, cool, shell, chop and set aside.

Meanwhile, trim the asparagus: snap or cut off any woody ends from the stems. Put in a covered saucepan with a small amount of water and steam for about 10 minutes, or until tender and still bright green, depending on the thickness. The tip of a sharp knife should glide easily into the thickest part of the stem when cooked. Drain well and toss with olive oil, salt and pepper, then sprinkle the chopped eggs and Parmesan shavings over the top.

4 eggs

500 g asparagus

4 tablespoons olive oil

75 g Parmesan, shaved with a vegetable peeler

salt and black pepper

hearty mains

stir-fried *tofu* with crisp *greens* and *mushrooms*

This stir-fry is very fresh and very Thai in its simplicity and balance of flavours. You will only need to quickly cook the greens in boiling water to soften them a little, which will also bring out their brilliant emerald green colour. The mushrooms, available from any speciality Asian food shop, are a fantastic storecupboard staple – they are inexpensive and will keep indefinitely in an airtight container. The trick with drying out the tofu on kitchen paper is one you can use for other recipes using soft tofu and is especially good for fried tofu dishes.

serves
4

300 g soft tofu, cut into 2–3-cm cubes

8 dried Chinese mushrooms

50 g sugar snap peas, trimmed

50 g mangetout, trimmed

2 bunches of fine asparagus, cut into 4-cm lengths

65 ml vegetable oil

2 garlic cloves, crushed

1 tablespoon light soy sauce

a pinch of white or black pepper

a pinch of sugar

Put the tofu on several layers of kitchen paper and leave for 20–30 minutes to absorb excess moisture. Put the mushrooms in a heatproof bowl and cover with boiling water. Set aside for 20 minutes. Drain the mushrooms, remove the stems and halve any larger ones.

Blanch the vegetables in boiling water for 30 seconds, until bright emerald green and softened. Drain and cover with cold water to stop them cooking further. When cold, drain well.

Heat a wok over high heat, then add the oil. Cook the tofu cubes in the hot oil for 5 minutes, turning often, until light golden and puffed. Transfer the tofu to kitchen paper and pour off all but 2 tablespoons of oil from the wok.

Add the vegetables to the wok and stir-fry for 2 minutes. Add the mushrooms and gently stir-fry for 1 minute. Add the garlic and stir-fry for 1 minute, then add the soy sauce, pepper, sugar and 2 tablespoons water to the wok. Return the tofu to the wok and stir-fry gently for 1 minute to coat all the ingredients in the sauce, being careful not to break up the tofu. Remove the wok from the heat and serve with steamed jasmine rice, if you like.

stir-fried *vegetables* with *five-spice tofu*

½ teaspoon Chinese
five-spice powder

250 g firm tofu, cut into
2-cm cubes

2 tablespoons vegetable oil

3 garlic cloves, crushed

200 g small broccoli florets

200 g pak choi, sliced

200 g mangetout

1 large carrot, cut into
matchsticks

1 red pepper, deseeded and
cut into matchsticks

85 g tinned water chestnuts,
drained and sliced

85 g tinned sliced bamboo
shoots, drained and rinsed

Sauce

2 tablespoons oyster sauce

2 tablespoons light soy sauce

125 ml vegetable stock

1 tablespoon cornflour,
combined with 2 tablespoons
cold water

serves
4

Q

This is a hearty and flavoursome vegetarian dish, called
Buddha's delight, traditionally eaten on the first day of Chinese
New Year – Buddhists believe that meat should not be eaten on
the first five days of the year. Every Buddhist family has their
own version and ingredients vary from cook to cook.

Combine all the sauce ingredients in a bowl and set aside.

Sprinkle the five-spice powder over the tofu.

Heat the oil in a wok or large frying pan until hot. Add the tofu in batches
and stir-fry over high heat until golden all over. Remove the tofu from the
wok and drain well on kitchen paper.

Add the garlic to the hot wok and stir-fry for 1 minute, or until golden. Add
the broccoli, pak choi, mangetout, carrot and red pepper with a sprinkle of
water and stir-fry over high heat for 2–3 minutes. Finally, throw in the water
chestnuts and bamboo shoots.

Pour the sauce into the wok and bring to the boil, then reduce the heat and
simmer gently for 2 minutes, or until the sauce has thickened. Divide
between 4 bowls and serve with rice or noodles.

1 tablespoon sesame oil

1 onion, sliced

200 g green beans, halved

350 g deep-fried tofu, sliced

2 tablespoons sweet chilli sauce

a handful of basil leaves

2 tablespoons sesame seeds, toasted in a dry frying pan

Chilli coconut sauce

1 lemongrass stalk

400 ml coconut milk

300 ml vegetable stock

1 tablespoon Thai fish sauce (see Introduction, right)

8 lime leaves, sliced

2 garlic cloves, chopped

3 cm fresh ginger, peeled and grated

4 tablespoons sunflower oil

4 eggs, lightly beaten

150 g dried thick rice noodles, soaked in warm water for 5 minutes, then drained

100 g kale or other leafy green, tough central core removed and leaves chopped

2 tablespoons lime juice

4 tablespoons sweet chilli sauce

4 tablespoons light soy sauce

1 large carrot, grated

100 g beansprouts

To serve

50 g roasted peanuts, chopped

4 spring onions, finely sliced

a handful of coriander

stir-fried *tofu* with *chilli coconut* sauce

serves 4

Deep-fried tofu is available from Asian shops or health food stores where they can be found in the refrigerator. You can substitute ordinary firm tofu, cut into cubes instead. If you are strictly vegetarian and will not eat fish sauce, you can buy a vegetarian 'fish' sauce which is made from soya beans. If you can't find it, use light soy sauce as a substitute.

To make the chilli coconut sauce, snap the lemongrass stalk in half. Put it, with all the other sauce ingredients, in a saucepan. Bring to the boil and simmer for 20 minutes until reduced by half. Strain the sauce and reserve.

Heat the oil in a wok or frying pan and stir-fry the onions and beans for 1 minute, add the tofu and stir-fry for a further 1 minute. Add the coconut sauce, sweet chilli sauce and basil leaves and heat through. Serve sprinkled with the sesame seeds.

pad thai *noodles*

serves 4

Q

Pad Thai is probably the best-known of all Thai noodle dishes and it takes only 5 minutes to cook. Use thick ribbon-like rice noodles ('rice sticks') for authenticity, or rice vermicelli or egg noodles. The best thing about this dish is that you can use almost anything as the base for it, so if you are feeding meat-eating friends, you can add some chopped, cooked chicken or even prawns to their portion.

Heat a wok until very hot, then add the oil. Add the eggs and noodles and stir-fry for about 2 minutes, until the eggs are lightly scrambled. Add the remaining ingredients and stir-fry for a further 3–5 minutes, until the noodles are cooked. Divide between 4 warmed bowls and serve sprinkled with the peanuts, spring onions and coriander.

stir-fried mushrooms

stir-fried tofu with chilli coconut sauce

stir-fried *mushrooms*

Try to use an assortment of mushrooms in this recipe. They are cooked here with the famous 'Chinese Trinity' of stir-fry tastes – aromatic garlic, ginger and spring onions.

Clean the mushrooms with a soft cloth and trim the stems if necessary. Chop the larger mushrooms in half.

Heat the oil in a wok. Add the garlic, ginger and spring onions and stir-fry for about 20 seconds, then add the firmer kinds of mushrooms. Stir-fry for a few minutes, add the sugar and soy sauce and stir-fry quickly until the sugar is dissolved. Add the softer mushrooms, turning gently in the sauce without breaking them up. Transfer to a serving plate and serve with rice or noodles.

1 kg assorted mushrooms

2 tablespoons vegetable oil

2 garlic cloves, crushed

2.5 cm fresh ginger, peeled and grated

6 spring onions, finely sliced

1 teaspoon sugar

2 teaspoons dark soy sauce

250 g egg noodles

2 tablespoons sunflower oil

2 garlic cloves, chopped

1 tablespoon red curry paste
(see Introduction, right)

80 g oyster mushrooms, sliced

2 small celery stalks, finely
chopped

100 g baby sweetcorn, halved
lengthways

80 g beansprouts

3 spring onions, thinly sliced

2 tomatoes, cut into wedges

3 tablespoons light soy sauce

1 teaspoon sugar

2 tablespoons sunflower oil

1 red onion, chopped

1 large red pepper, deseeded
and chopped

2 garlic cloves

2 teaspoons ground coriander

1 teaspoon ground cumin

½ teaspoon ground cinnamon

400 g sweet potatoes, cubed

400-g tin chopped tomatoes

400-g tin red kidney beans,
rinsed and drained

2 teaspoons sweet chilli sauce

15–25 g dark chocolate, grated

salt and black pepper

egg noodles stir-fried with *vegetables* and *red curry paste*

This quick stir-fry mélange is widely popular because it offers something to suit almost any taste. The curry paste provides the hot flavour and the vegetables add a wholesome crispness. Be aware that some brands of red curry paste contain traces of seafood. However, there are many vegetarian-friendly brands so just check the ingredients carefully before you choose one.

Cook the noodles according to the instructions on the packet. Drain well.

Heat the oil in a wok. Add the garlic, fry for about 1 minute, then add the curry paste and continue stir-frying until the garlic is golden. Add the noodles, stir well, then add the remaining ingredients. Stir-fry for a couple of minutes.

quick mexican *mole*

serves 4

Although it may sound unusual, chocolate is the secret ingredient of this Mexican-inspired dish. It adds a wonderfully rich, intense flavour to the vegetables. Serve with boiled rice or a chunk of crusty bread.

Heat the oil in a saucepan and fry the onion, pepper, garlic and spices for 5 minutes. Add the sweet potatoes, tomatoes, beans, chilli sauce and 300 ml water and bring to the boil. Cover and simmer gently for 30 minutes.

Stir in the chocolate and cook for a final 5 minutes. Taste and adjust the seasoning with salt and pepper, then serve.

egg noodles stir-fried with
vegetables and red curry paste

spinach and *cheese* curry

This is a fabulous vegetarian-friendly curry made with paneer, a firm, fresh white Indian cheese. It's not that easy to find but as luck would have it, halloumi, a cheese from Cyprus, works just as well. The other ingredients are all readily available. Try to have a jar of shop-bought curry paste on standby in the fridge – it keeps well and saves you from having a cupboard full of dry spices which have a short shelf life. Serve with cooked basmati rice.

serves
4

Q

1 tablespoon vegetable oil

250 g paneer or halloumi, cut into 2-cm cubes

2 tablespoons butter

2 tablespoons mild Indian curry paste (Madras or balti)

2 large green chillies (optional), deseeded and chopped

500 g spinach, roughly chopped

a handful of coriander, leaves and stems freshly chopped

125 ml single cream

lemon wedges, to serve

Heat the oil in a non-stick frying pan over high heat and cook the cubes of cheese for 2–3 minutes, turning often, until golden all over. Remove the cheese to a plate and set aside until needed.

Add the butter to the pan and when sizzling hot, add the curry paste and green chillies and stir-fry for 2 minutes. Add the spinach and coriander and cook for 1–2 minutes, until all the spinach has wilted, then stir in the cream.

Add the cheese and cook over low heat for 2–3 minutes, to warm the cheese through. Serve the curry with lemon wedges to squeeze over the top and cooked basmati rice.

quick *vegetable* curry

serves 4

3 tablespoons sunflower oil

1 onion, sliced

2 garlic cloves, chopped

3 cm fresh ginger, peeled and grated

1 tablespoon hot curry paste

1 teaspoon ground cinnamon

500 g potatoes, cubed

400-g tin chopped tomatoes

300 ml vegetable stock

1 tablespoon tomato purée

200 g button mushrooms, halved

200 g peas (fresh or frozen)

25 g ground almonds

2 tablespoons freshly chopped coriander

salt and black pepper

If you're into fast cooking, this is the ultimate cheat's curry, made with ready-made curry paste. Serve with basmati rice and warm naan bread, if you like. It might strike you as odd to use ground almonds in a curry but in fact it makes the sauce lovely and creamy, without the heaviness of cream itself. Why don't you use your leftover ground almonds for one of the puddings in the last chapter of this book?

Heat the oil in a large saucepan and fry the onion, garlic, ginger, curry paste and cinnamon for 5 minutes. Add the potatoes, tomatoes, stock, tomato purée, salt and pepper. Bring to the boil, cover and simmer gently for 20 minutes.

Add the mushrooms, peas, ground almonds and coriander to the pan and cook for a further 10 minutes. Taste and adjust the seasoning with salt and pepper, then serve with basmati rice.

cauliflower masala

serves 4

1 tablespoon sunflower oil

2 teaspoons cumin seeds

500 g cauliflower florets

2 garlic cloves, thinly sliced

2 cm fresh ginger, peeled and finely chopped

1 green chilli, thinly sliced

1 teaspoon garam masala

150 ml hot water

juice of ½ lemon

salt and black pepper

In this Indian-inspired recipe, cauliflower florets are stir-fried in a seasoned, spiced oil until just tender. Substitute broccoli florets if you like, to ring the changes.

Heat the sunflower oil in a large frying pan over medium heat. Add the cumin seeds. Stir-fry for 30 seconds, then add the cauliflower, garlic, ginger and chilli. Turn the heat to high and stir-fry for 6–8 minutes, or until the cauliflower is lightly browned at the edges.

Stir in the garam masala and hot water and stir well. Cover and cook over high heat for 1–2 minutes.

Season well and drizzle with the lemon juice just before serving.

quick vegetable curry

fresh *tomato, pea* and *paneer* curry

This is such a great, fresh-tasting curry to cook for a small group. It's a real get-stuck-in kind of meal, best enjoyed with lots of accompaniments on the side, like basmati rice, warm naan bread, mango chutney and maybe even a raita from page 20. As with the Spinach and Cheese Curry on page 115, if you can't find paneer, halloumi is a perfectly good replacement.

serves
4

Heat the oil in a frying pan over medium heat. Add the paneer and cook for 4–5 minutes, turning often, until golden all over. Remove from the pan and set aside.

Add the butter to the pan. When it is melted and sizzling, add the onions and stir-fry until softened and lightly golden. Add the ginger and chillies to the pan and cook for 1 minute. Add the tomatoes, vinegar and 65 ml water and bring to the boil. Cook for about 5 minutes, to thicken slightly. Add the peas and return the paneer to the pan. Reduce the heat and simmer for about 5 minutes, until the peas are tender.

Stir in the garam masala and season to taste with salt and pepper. Sprinkle with the coriander leaves and serve with basmati rice and an assortment of Indian accompaniments.

2 tablespoons vegetable oil

250 g paneer, cubed

1 tablespoon butter

2 onions, finely chopped

5 cm fresh ginger, peeled and grated

2 green chillies, deseeded and finely chopped

3 ripe tomatoes, chopped

2 teaspoons white wine vinegar

200 g frozen peas

½ teaspoon garam masala

a handful of coriander leaves

salt and black pepper

mustardy mushroom stroganoff

150 ml vegetable stock

½ small onion, sliced

150 g mixed mushrooms, chopped if large

1 garlic clove, crushed

1 teaspoon (preferably) grainy mustard

½ teaspoon tomato purée

1 tablespoon crème fraîche

salt and black pepper

freshly chopped parsley, to serve (optional)

serves 1 | **Q**

For nights when you want dinner in a hurry, this can be on the table in just 10 minutes. Serve with basmati and wild rice (which is really good for you!) or couscous, together with some green beans or cabbage.

Put 3 tablespoons of the stock in a saucepan. Add the onion, cover the pan and cook for about 4 minutes or until the onion has softened and the liquid has evaporated.

Stir in the mushrooms, garlic and some salt and pepper, then add the remaining stock, mustard and tomato purée. Cook, covered, for 2 minutes, then remove the lid and cook rapidly for 2 minutes to reduce the liquid to a syrup. Stir in the crème fraîche and parsley, if using, and serve immediately with rice or couscous.

red kidney bean curry

1 tablespoon butter

2 tablespoons sunflower oil

1 onion, finely chopped

½ teaspoon ground cinnamon

2 dried bay leaves

3 garlic cloves, crushed

2 cm fresh ginger, peeled and finely chopped

½ teaspoon ground turmeric

1 teaspoon ground coriander

2 teaspoons ground cumin

1 teaspoon garam masala

2 dried red chillies

400-g tin red kidney beans

4 tablespoons tomato purée

salt and black pepper

serves 4 | **Q**

A lightly spiced bean curry, this is yummy comfort food, and ready in a matter of minutes. Serve with cooked basmati rice.

Heat the butter and sunflower oil in a large, heavy-based saucepan and add the onion, cinnamon, bay leaves, garlic and ginger. Stir-fry for 4–5 minutes. Stir in the turmeric, ground coriander, cumin, garam masala and chillies.

Add the beans, tomato purée and a little water to make a thick sauce. Bring to the boil and cook for 4–5 minutes, stirring often. Season well and serve.

mustardy mushroom
stroganoff

ratatouille

ratatouille

Ratatouille is a celebration of summer. It's best made when courgettes, aubergines and tomatoes are in season so that you get the best flavour. Serve it warm with rice or couscous – it's so good it's guaranteed to please even non-vegetarians.

serves
6

Heat the oil in a large, heavy-based saucepan over medium heat. Add the onion, garlic and parsley and sauté for 10 minutes, stirring regularly.

Add the aubergine and cook for 5 minutes. Add the peppers and courgettes and stir in the salt. Cook for a few minutes, then add the chopped tomatoes.

Cover and cook for 5 minutes until the tomatoes start to break down, then uncover and cook for 10–15 minutes until the vegetables are tender, adding a little water if necessary. Season to taste with vinegar, if using, and salt and pepper. Serve warm.

3 tablespoons olive oil

1 onion, sliced

3 garlic cloves, crushed

a small handful of parsley, freshly chopped

1 large aubergine, chopped

2–3 red and/or yellow peppers, deseeded and chopped

4 courgettes, sliced

¼ teaspoon salt

400-g tin chopped tomatoes

2 teaspoons red wine vinegar or balsamic vinegar (optional)

salt and black pepper

lemon and *spinach puy lentils* with hard-boiled *eggs*

Puy lentils have a slightly firm texture and nutty flavour, and retain their shape when cooked, unlike other lentils.

serves
2–3

Hard-boil the eggs following the instructions in the Avocado and Chickpea Salad recipe on page 45. Drain, cool, shell, halve and set aside.

Put the lentils and bay leaf in a saucepan. Cover with cold water and bring to the boil. Reduce the heat, half-cover the pan and cook for 25–30 minutes until tender but not mushy. Drain the lentils and set aside.

Meanwhile, heat the oil in a frying pan and fry the onion, covered, for 10 minutes until softened. Add the tomatoes and spinach to the pan and cook, stirring, for another 2 minutes until the spinach has wilted.

Add the cooked lentils to the pan with the mustard, crème fraîche and lemon juice, stirring until everything is combined. Season to taste and warm through. Spoon the lentils onto plates and top with the hard-boiled eggs.

2–3 large eggs

140 g Puy or green lentils, rinsed

1 dried bay leaf

1 tablespoon olive oil

1 large onion, chopped

5 tomatoes, deseeded and cut into chunks

150 g spinach, chopped

2 teaspoons mustard

2 tablespoons crème fraîche

juice of 1 lemon

salt and black pepper

spiced *aubergine* couscous

65 ml vegetable oil

1 large aubergine, cubed

1 tablespoon olive oil

280 g couscous

½ teaspoon paprika

½ teaspoon chilli powder

375 ml vegetable stock

a small handful of coriander, leaves and stems freshly chopped

50–60 g baby spinach

125 ml natural yoghurt

lemon wedges, to serve

serves 4

Popping its head up in just about every style of cuisine, aubergine is very versatile – see the Ratatouille on the previous page, or the Baked Aubergines with Garlic and Tomatoes on page 127. It is just as much at home steamed with spring onions and fresh ginger as it is with tomato, basil and cheese or, as in this dish, with Moroccan spices. You will need one large aubergine, so look for one that is firm, full and heavy with shiny deep-purple skin. The couscous recipe alone is a treat and can be made on its own for any other occasion.

Heat the vegetable oil in a frying pan over high heat and cook the aubergine for 3–4 minutes, turning often so it is an even, golden brown all over. Place on kitchen paper to drain off the excess oil.

Heat the olive oil in a saucepan over medium heat. Add the couscous, paprika and chilli powder and cook for 2 minutes, stirring constantly. Add the stock and bring to the boil. Remove the pan from the heat, cover with a tight-fitting lid and leave to stand for 10 minutes.

Fluff the couscous with a fork, then cover and leave for a further 5 minutes. Place the couscous in a large bowl and add the aubergine, coriander and baby spinach and toss to combine.

Place on a plate with the yoghurt and lemon wedges on the side to serve.

Variation Replace the aubergine with sliced courgettes. Pan-fry them in a little olive oil until golden on both sides. Add the courgettes to the prepared couscous with a handful of freshly chopped mint.

baked *aubergines* with *garlic* and *tomatoes*

This is a traditional, summery Turkish dish called 'imam bayildi'. The aubergines are halved, filled with simple ingredients, and then baked slowly until they are soft and bursting with flavour. This is easy enough for a casual dinner at home (remembering that the aubergines will need 45 minutes in the oven) but also special enough for when you have friends round.

serves
4

Heat half the olive oil in a large frying pan, add the aubergine and shallow-fry, turning them over until light golden on both sides, about 10–15 minutes. (Fry in batches if your frying pan is too small.) Remove and drain on kitchen paper. Arrange the pieces side by side in an ovenproof dish and season with salt and pepper.

Preheat the oven to 190°C (375°F) Gas 5.

To make the stuffing, heat the remaining olive oil in a saucepan, add the onion and sauté gently until it starts to colour. Add the garlic and cumin and fry for 2–3 minutes. Add the tomatoes, oregano, some salt and pepper, the sugar and 100 ml water, then cover with a lid and cook for 15 minutes, stirring occasionally.

Stir in the parsley, then divide the stuffing into 4 equal portions. Pile each portion along the length of each aubergine half. Add the diluted tomato purée to the base of the dish and cook in the preheated oven for 45 minutes, basting the aubergines once during cooking. Serve hot or warm.

100 ml olive oil

2 medium aubergines, rinsed and halved lengthways

salt and black pepper

Stuffing

1 onion, finely chopped

2 garlic cloves, crushed

½ teaspoon ground cumin

350 g ripe tomatoes, chopped

2 teaspoons dried oregano

½ teaspoon sugar

2 tablespoons freshly chopped parsley

2 teaspoons tomato purée, diluted with 100 ml hot water

roasted early autumn *vegetables* with *chickpeas*

serves 4

12 small mushrooms

2 ripe tomatoes, halved

1 red pepper, deseeded and cut into strips

1 yellow pepper, deseeded and cut into strips

1 red onion, cut into wedges

1 small fennel bulb, sliced into thin wedges

1 whole garlic bulb, broken into individual cloves but left unpeeled

2 teaspoons salt

2 tablespoons olive oil

400-g tin chickpeas, drained and rinsed

2 thyme or rosemary sprigs

This is no-fuss cooking at its best. Throw a few tasty vegetables into a roomy roasting tin, chuck in a lot of garlic and a tin of chickpeas – for protein – and you have yourself the makings of a great Saturday supper. The garlic cloves turn soft and sweet in their skins so make sure you squeeze out and enjoy the flesh. It's delicious! Serve this winning meal with couscous, which always seems to like being with slow-roasted Mediterranean veg.

Preheat the oven to 180°C (350°F) Gas 4.

Put the mushrooms, tomatoes, red and yellow peppers, onion, fennel and garlic bulbs in a large roasting tin. Sprinkle the salt evenly over the vegetables and drizzle with the oil. Toss well to coat. Roast in the preheated oven for 1 hour.

Remove the roasting tin from the oven and turn the vegetables. Add the chickpeas and thyme sprigs. Return the tin to the oven and roast for a further 30 minutes, until the edges of the vegetables are just starting to blacken and char. Serve with couscous, if you like.

orange *vegetable* and *spring onion* pilau

This technique of cooking rice is Middle Eastern in origin but it has spread far and wide – similar rice dishes can be found in European, Asian, Latin American, Caribbean and Indian cuisines, and it is known by many names including pilaf, pilav and pulao. It's one of those surprisingly satisfying recipes that you will come back to again and again – perfect bowl food for gobbling up on the sofa in front of the television.

serves
4

Put the oil in a heavy-based saucepan set over high heat. Add the onion, garlic, ginger and chilli and cook for 5 minutes, stirring often. Add the spices and almonds and cook for a further 5 minutes, until the spices become aromatic and look very dark in the pan.

Add the rice and cook for a minute, stirring well to coat the rice in the spices. Add the carrot, pumpkin and sweet potato to the pan. Pour in 600 ml water and stir well, loosening any grains of rice that are stuck to the bottom of the pan. Bring to the boil, then reduce the heat to low, cover with a tight-fitting lid and cook for 25 minutes, stirring occasionally.

Add the lime juice and coriander, stir well to combine and serve.

2 tablespoons olive oil

1 onion, chopped

2 garlic cloves, chopped

5 cm fresh ginger, peeled and finely chopped

1 large red chilli, finely chopped

1 teaspoon ground coriander

1 teaspoon ground cumin

1 teaspoon turmeric

50 g flaked almonds

300 g basmati rice

1 carrot, cut into large chunks

200 g pumpkin or squash, peeled, deseeded and cut into wedges

1 small sweet potato, cut into thick half-circles

juice of 1 lime

a handful of coriander, freshly chopped

broccoli and *lemon* risotto

serves
4

900 ml vegetable stock

50 g unsalted butter

1 tablespoon olive oil

8 shallots, finely chopped

2 garlic cloves, crushed

275 g risotto rice

1 glass of white wine, about 125 ml

275 g purple sprouting broccoli, chopped, or broccoli florets

1 small red pepper, deseeded and diced

100 g Parmesan, grated

grated zest of 2 lemons

a handful of parsley, freshly chopped

salt and black pepper

Risottos are ideal vegetarian fare. Make sure you buy real risotto rice, and don't skimp on the Parmesan or white wine (you can always enjoy the rest of the wine with your meal!) – these are the things that make a risotto so tasty. Purple sprouting broccoli is what you really want in this recipe – it has a delicious nutty flavour – but don't worry if you can't find it. Just use broccoli instead.

Put the stock in a large saucepan. Heat until almost boiling, then reduce the heat until barely simmering to keep it hot.

Heat the butter and oil in a large saucepan over medium heat. Add the shallots and cook for 1–2 minutes, until softened but not browned. Add the garlic and mix well.

Add the rice and stir, using a wooden spoon, until the grains are well coated and glistening, about 1 minute. Pour in the wine and stir until it has been completely absorbed.

Add 1 ladle of hot stock and simmer, stirring until it has been absorbed. Repeat. After 10 minutes, add the broccoli and red pepper. Continue to add the stock at intervals and cook as before, for a further 8–10 minutes, until the liquid has been absorbed and the broccoli and rice are tender but still firm (al dente).

Add the Parmesan, lemon zest, parsley and some salt and pepper. Mix well. Remove from the heat, cover and leave to rest for 2 minutes.

Spoon into bowls and serve immediately.

roasted *butternut squash* risotto

This is quite a special risotto. It doesn't need much effort, or even any fancy ingredients, but it looks and tastes so good that you think it must have required a lot of work. In fact, the secret to its success is roasting the squash first, which brings out its sweetness, while the pumpkin seeds add a spicy crunch.

serves 2

500 g butternut squash, peeled, deseeded and diced

3 tablespoons olive oil

1½ teaspoons dried chilli flakes

25 g pumpkin seeds

850 ml vegetable stock

1 small onion, finely chopped

150 g risotto rice

100 ml white wine

50 g Parmesan, grated

salt and black pepper

crème fraîche, to serve

Preheat the oven to 230°C (450°F) Gas 8.

Put the butternut squash in a small roasting tin with 1 tablespoon of the olive oil and ½ teaspoon of the chilli flakes and season well. Toss the squash in the seasoned oil until it is evenly coated. Roast in the preheated oven for about 20 minutes, or until soft and golden. (Use a large spoon to turn the squash at regular intervals while it is cooking.)

Heat 1 tablespoon of the remaining olive oil in a small frying pan and toast the pumpkin seeds with the remaining chilli flakes for about 1–2 minutes until lightly browned. Set aside until needed.

While the squash is cooking in the oven, make the risotto. Put the stock in a saucepan. Heat until almost boiling, then reduce the heat until barely simmering to keep it hot.

Pour the remaining oil into a saucepan and gently fry the onion over medium heat for about 1 minute, or until softened. Add the rice, stir for 2–3 minutes, then add the wine and simmer until reduced by half. Add another ladleful of hot stock. Let the risotto continue to simmer gently, adding another ladleful or two of stock each time the liquid has been absorbed into the rice. Stir, almost continuously, until the rice has absorbed all the stock.

Once the rice is cooked and tender, stir in the roasted butternut squash and Parmesan and season to taste. Serve immediately, topped with a little crème fraîche and sprinkled with the toasted pumpkin seeds.

farmers' risotto

serves 4

When you can't decide what to cook, look to the vegetables in your fridge for inspiration – they're usually suitable for a risotto. This one is easy to make and you can use any vegetable you like. Just remember to cut them into neat, equal-sized pieces for even cooking.

900 ml vegetable stock

50 g unsalted butter

1 tablespoon olive oil

8 shallots, finely chopped

1 garlic clove, crushed

275 g risotto rice

75 ml white wine

1 small courgette, finely chopped

2–3 firm tomatoes, deseeded and finely chopped

50 g green beans, finely chopped

1 small leek, thinly sliced

100 g Parmesan, grated

2 tablespoons single cream

a small handful of parsley, freshly chopped

a small handful of basil, leaves torn

salt and black pepper

Put the stock in a saucepan. Heat until almost boiling, then reduce the heat until barely simmering to keep it hot.

Heat the butter and oil in a large saucepan over medium heat. Add the shallots and cook for 1–2 minutes, until softened but not browned. Add the garlic and mix well.

Add the rice and stir until the grains are well coated and glistening, about 1 minute. Pour in the wine and stir until it has been completely absorbed.

Add 1 ladle of hot stock and simmer, stirring until it has been absorbed. Repeat. After 10 minutes, add all the vegetables and mix well. Continue to add stock at intervals and cook as before, for a further 8–10 minutes, until the liquid has been absorbed and the vegetables and rice are tender but still firm (al dente).

Mix in the Parmesan, cream, herbs and some salt and pepper. Remove from the heat, cover and leave to rest for 2 minutes before serving.

mushroom risotto

serves
6

Any kind of fresh wild mushroom will make this taste wonderful — but wild mushrooms can be very expensive, so the cheat's trick is to use a mixture of cultivated mushrooms, plus a small amount of dried porcini mushrooms. Dried porcini are one of those useful storecupboard ingredients that add flavour to many recipes. You need to soak them in hot water before using, to rejuvenate them.

Put the dried porcini mushrooms in a small bowl, cover with warm water and set aside for 20 minutes. Drain and chop.

Clean the fresh, assorted mushrooms with a soft cloth and trim the stems if necessary. Chop the larger mushrooms in half.

Put the stock in a saucepan and keep at a gentle simmer. Melt the butter in a large, heavy saucepan and add the onion and garlic. Cook gently for 10 minutes until softened but not browned. Stir in the mushrooms and herbs, then cook over medium heat for 3 minutes to heat through. Pour in the wine and stir until it has been completely absorbed. Stir in the rice and fry with the onion and mushrooms until slightly opaque.

Begin adding the stock, a large ladle at a time, stirring until each ladle has been absorbed by the rice. Continue until the rice is tender and creamy, but the grains still firm (al dente), about 18–20 minutes.

Taste and season well with salt and pepper. Stir in the Parmesan, cover and leave to rest for a couple of minutes before serving. Serve immediately with extra grated Parmesan.

25 g dried porcini

200 g assorted mushrooms

900 ml vegetable stock

125 g unsalted butter

1 large onion, finely chopped

2 garlic cloves, finely chopped

1 teaspoon dried thyme

1 glass of white wine, about 150 ml

450 g risotto rice

75 g Parmesan, grated, plus extra to serve

salt and black pepper

country-style risotto

serves 4

900 ml vegetable stock

2 tablespoons olive oil

2 garlic cloves, crushed

100 g pumpkin flesh, diced

2 ripe plum tomatoes, deseeded and chopped

50 g peas (fresh or frozen)

10 green beans, chopped

1 small courgette, chopped

100 g unsalted butter

8 shallots, finely chopped

1 carrot, finely chopped

2 celery stalks, finely chopped

a handful of parsley, freshly chopped

275 g risotto rice

1 glass of white wine, about 125 ml

100 g Parmesan, grated

salt and black pepper

This is the kind of hearty risotto you want on a cold wintry evening. Cook the vegetables in a separate pan (to retain their individual flavours and textures), then add them to the risotto. If you don't want to use pumpkin, or it's not in season, you can use broccoli instead.

Put the stock in a saucepan. Heat until almost boiling, then reduce the heat until barely simmering to keep it hot.

Heat 1 tablespoon of the olive oil in a frying pan and add the garlic, pumpkin, tomatoes, peas, green beans and courgette. Cook until just tender, about 8 minutes, then remove and set aside.

Heat half the butter and the remaining oil in a large saucepan over medium heat. Add the shallots, carrot, celery and parsley and cook for 1–2 minutes, until softened but not browned.

Add the rice and stir until the grains are well coated and glistening, about 1 minute. Pour in the wine and stir until it has been completely absorbed.

Add 1 ladle of hot stock and simmer, stirring until it has been absorbed. Continue to add the stock at intervals and cook as before, until the liquid has been absorbed and the rice is tender but still firm (al dente), about 18–20 minutes. Reserve the last ladle of stock.

Add the reserved stock and cooked vegetables, and some salt and pepper. Mix well. Stir in the Parmesan and remaining butter. Mix well. Remove from the heat, cover and leave to rest for 2 minutes before serving.

spinach risotto with *rocket* and roasted *tomatoes*

This simple risotto makes the most of young spinach and peppery rocket, but watercress makes a good alternative if you can't find rocket. Roasting the tomatoes first means that this is not a last-minute risotto, but is does make the tomotoes lovely and sweet, so it's well worth the extra time.

Preheat the oven to 200°C (400°F) Gas 6.

Put the tomatoes in a roasting tin and drizzle with olive oil. Mix well to coat, then season with salt and pepper. Roast in the preheated oven for about 20 minutes or until slightly collapsed with the skins beginning to brown. Remove from the oven and set aside.

Put the stock and soy sauce in a saucepan. Heat until almost boiling, then reduce the heat until barely simmering to keep it hot.

Melt half the butter in a large, heavy saucepan and add the onion. Cook gently for 10 minutes until softened but not browned. Add the rice and stir until well coated with the butter and heated through. Pour in the wine and stir until it has been completely absorbed. Remove from the heat.

Return the risotto to the heat, warm through and begin adding the stock, a large ladle at a time, stirring gently until each ladle has been almost absorbed into the rice. Continue until the rice is tender and creamy, but the grains still firm (al dente), about 18–20 minutes.

Just before the risotto is cooked, stir in the spinach and rocket. Taste and season well with salt and pepper and beat in the remaining butter and the Parmesan. You may like to add a little more hot stock to the risotto at this stage to loosen it.

Cover and leave to rest for 2 minutes. Fold in the tomatoes and their juices then serve immediately.

serves
4

400 g cherry tomatoes

4 tablespoons olive oil

900 ml vegetable stock

a dash of soy sauce

125 g unsalted butter

1 onion, finely chopped

275 g risotto rice

1 glass of white wine, about 150 ml

200 g young spinach leaves

50 g rocket leaves

salt and black pepper

grated Parmesan, to serve

tomato risotto

900 ml vegetable stock

50 g unsalted butter

1 tablespoon olive oil

8 shallots, finely chopped

2 garlic cloves, crushed

275 g risotto rice

8 firm tomatoes, deseeded and coarsely chopped

100 g Parmesan, grated

a large handful of basil, leaves torn

salt and black pepper

serves
4

Try to find really tasty tomatoes for this risotto – since they are the main ingredient, they need to be full of flavour otherwise the risotto will end up bland. The combination of tomatoes, basil and Parmesan is deliciously Italian.

Put the stock in a saucepan. Heat until almost boiling, then reduce the heat until barely simmering to keep it hot.

Heat the butter and oil in a large saucepan over medium heat. Add the shallots and cook for 1–2 minutes, until softened but not browned. Add the garlic and mix well.

Add the rice and stir until the grains are well coated and glistening, about 1 minute. Pour in the wine and stir until it has been completely absorbed.

Add 1 ladle of hot stock and simmer, stirring until it has been absorbed. Repeat. After 10 minutes, add the tomatoes. Continue to add the stock at intervals and cook as before, for a further 8–10 minutes, until the liquid has been absorbed and the tomatoes and rice are tender but still firm (al dente). Reserve the last ladle of stock.

Stir in the reserved stock, Parmesan, basil and some salt and pepper. Remove from the heat, cover and leave to rest for 2 minutes before serving.

risotto with *lemon* and *mint*

Sometimes you don't want a heavy risotto packed with ingredients. This is a wonderfully light and fresh-tasting option with the sunshine flavours of lemon and mint. It requires so few ingredients that it's good if you unexpectedly get hungry friends round for dinner.

serves
4

Put the stock in a saucepan. Heat until almost boiling, then reduce the heat until barely simmering to keep it hot.

Heat the butter and oil in a large saucepan over medium heat. Add the shallots and cook for 1–2 minutes, until softened but not browned. Add the garlic and mix well.

Add the rice and stir until the grains are well coated and glistening, about 1 minute. Pour in the wine and stir until it has been completely absorbed.

Add 1 ladle of hot stock and simmer, stirring until it has been absorbed. Continue to add the stock at intervals and cook as before, until the liquid has been absorbed and the rice is tender but firm (al dente), about 18–20 minutes.

Stir in the Parmesan, lemon zest, cream, mint and some salt and pepper. Remove from the heat, cover and leave to rest for 2 minutes before serving.

900 ml vegetable stock

50 g unsalted butter

1 tablespoon olive oil

8 shallots, finely chopped

1 garlic clove, crushed

275 g risotto rice

75 ml white wine

100 g Parmesan, grated

grated zest of 3 lemons

2 tablespoons single cream

a handful of mint, freshly chopped

salt and black pepper

vegetable burritos

400-g tin chopped tomatoes

3 garlic cloves, crushed

1 tablespoon mild chilli powder, or to taste

a pinch of dried oregano

1 tablespoon tomato purée

1 tablespoon olive oil

1 yellow pepper, deseeded and sliced

1 green pepper, deseeded and sliced

400-g tin refried beans (or borlotti or pinto beans, rinsed, drained and mashed)

4 soft flour or corn tortillas

100 g Cheddar, grated

2 tablespoons crème fraîche or soured cream

2 tablespoons freshly chopped coriander

salt and black pepper

Salsa

½ large red onion

2 tomatoes

½ green chilli, deseeded and finely chopped

1 tablespoon lime juice

1 tablespoon freshly chopped mint

serves
4

Q

Everyone loves burritos! They're the perfect TV dinner but that doesn't mean they have to be bad for you. These are made with yellow and green peppers and freshly made tomato salsa, and the refried beans are high in fibre. If there's a meat-eater among you, you can easily pan-fry some strips of chicken breast for them to add to their burrito filling.

Put the tomatoes in a saucepan with the garlic, chilli powder, oregano and tomato purée. Bring to the boil, reduce the heat and simmer for 10 minutes, until the mixture reduces slightly and begins to thicken.

Meanwhile, heat the oil in a separate saucepan. Add the peppers and sauté for about 5 minutes, until soft. Add the peppers to the tomato mixture.

Put the refried beans in another saucepan and heat gently, stirring frequently until piping hot.

To make the salsa, put all the ingredients in a small bowl and mix well.

Warm the tortillas according to the instructions on the packet.

Put the tortillas on 4 serving plates. Spread each tortilla with a thick layer of refried beans, then 1 tablespoon of the tomato and pepper mixture, 25 g cheese, 1 tablespoon of the salsa and ½ tablespoon crème fraîche. Sprinkle with coriander, fold and serve immediately.

huevos rancheros

These 'ranch eggs' are so brilliant because you can eat them at any time of day! They're often served up for breakfast or brunch, but they make an excellent choice for dinner or lunch too, because they're satisfying and filling. Unlike the Vegetable Burritos on page 148, the refried beans are home-made – you just need a tin of pinto or cannellini beans and Cheddar to make your own simple version. If you want to serve the huevos rancheros with a spoonful of guacamole or soured cream, that's a great idea, too.

serves
4

3 tablespoons vegetable oil

1 green chilli, deseeded and finely chopped

2 garlic cloves, crushed

500 g tomatoes, cut into slim wedges

400-g tin pinto or cannellini beans

50 g Cheddar, grated

juice of 1 lime, plus extra lime wedges to serve

a handful of coriander, freshly chopped

4 eggs

4 soft flour or corn tortillas

salt and black pepper

Heat 1 tablespoon of the oil in a large frying pan over medium heat, then add the chilli, half the garlic and a pinch of salt and fry for 1–2 minutes, until softened. Add the tomatoes and cook gently for about 20 minutes.

Heat the remaining oil in a small saucepan, add the remaining garlic and heat through for 20 seconds, until just browning. Add the beans, then using a potato masher, coarsely mash the beans and stir in plenty of salt and pepper and the Cheddar.

Stir the lime juice and coriander into the tomato sauce. Make 4 holes in the sauce and crack an egg into each one. Cook for 3 minutes until set. Cover with the lid for the last 30 seconds just to firm up the whites. Keep warm until needed.

Meanwhile, heat a frying pan over medium heat. Cook the tortillas for 1 minute on each side, until golden and hot. Transfer to 4 plates and spread the beans over the tortillas. Top with tomato salsa and the eggs. Serve with lime wedges and guacamole or soured cream if you like.

mozzarella-topped *herby vegetable* loaf

serves 3–4

This recipe is a bit like a veggie version of meatballs in tomato sauce. Eat it as it is or serve it with a little pasta or with new potatoes and peas or broccoli on the side.

240 g carrots, grated

1 red onion, finely chopped

2 garlic cloves, crushed

3 celery stalks, finely chopped

125 g mushrooms, sliced

1 small courgette, sliced

1 tablespoon freshly chopped parsley

2 tablespoons freshly chopped coriander

60 g Cheddar, grated

2 eggs

125 g wholemeal flour

150 g mozzarella, grated

Sauce

3 tablespoons olive oil

½ onion, sliced

1 garlic clove, crushed

2 x 400-g tins chopped tomatoes

1 teaspoon sugar

salt and black pepper

a 450-g loaf tin, lined with greaseproof paper

Preheat the oven to 180°C (350°F) Gas 4.

Mix the carrots, onion, garlic, celery, mushrooms, courgette, parsley, coriander, Cheddar, eggs and flour in a large bowl. Spoon the mixture into the prepared loaf tin and bake in the preheated oven for 1 hour.

Meanwhile, to make the sauce, heat the olive oil in a saucepan. Add the onion and garlic, cover with a lid and sweat over gentle heat until soft and pale golden.

Add the tinned tomatoes (with all the juice) to the onion mixture. Stir in the sugar and season to taste.

Cook, uncovered, for about 30 minutes, or until the tomato softens.

Remove the loaf from the oven and leave to stand for 5 minutes. Preheat the grill to hot.

Tip the loaf out onto a plate and slice. Put the slices into a shallow, ovenproof dish. Pour over the tomato sauce and sprinkle with the mozzarella. Grill for 4–5 minutes, or until the cheese is bubbling and golden. Serve immediately.

rice and *bean* burgers

There's something really satisfying about making your own burgers, especially when the finished product is superior to anything you might find in the shops. This recipe takes a little longer than you might expect but you will be rewarded with at least 5 meals (2 burgers per meal) for your labour. Pop any leftover burgers in the freezer before you cook them and take them out to defrost thoroughly as and when you need them.

makes
10

Cook the rice according to the instructions on the packet, allowing it to slightly overcook so that it is soft. Drain the rice, transfer it to a large bowl and reserve.

Put 2 tablespoons water and the Worcestershire sauce in a frying pan, add the onion and garlic and cook over medium heat until softened, about 8 minutes.

Put the onions, garlic, cooked rice, beans, breadcrumbs, egg, cheese and thyme in a blender or food processor. Add plenty of salt and pepper, then blend until combined. Alternatively, you can mash everything roughly in a bowl with a potato masher. Add the green pepper and grated carrot and mix well. Refrigerate the mixture for 1½ hours, or until quite firm.

Shape the mixture into 10 burgers, using wet hands if the mixture sticks. Coat them in flour or cornmeal and refrigerate for a further 30 minutes.

Heat the oil in a frying pan and fry the burgers for 3–4 minutes on each side, or until piping hot. Serve with salad leaves and relish.

Variation Add 1–2 deseeded finely chopped chillies to give an extra bite and 3 finely chopped celery stalks to add some crunch, if you like. Replace the thyme with freshly chopped coriander.

200 g brown rice
(not quick-cook variety)

2 tablespoons Worcestershire sauce

1 onion, chopped

2 garlic cloves, crushed

200-g tin cannellini beans, drained and rinsed

200-g tin red kidney beans, drained and rinsed

50 g breadcrumbs

1 egg, beaten

115 g Cheddar, grated

2 tablespoons freshly chopped thyme

1 small green pepper, deseeded and chopped

1 large carrot, coarsely grated

flour or cornmeal, for coating

2–3 tablespoons sunflower oil

salt and black pepper

salad leaves and relish, to serve (optional)

spiced *falafel* burgers

makes 8

225 g dried chickpeas (or use 400-g tin chickpeas and skip the overnight soaking step)

1 small onion, finely chopped

2 garlic cloves, crushed

½ handful of parsley, freshly chopped

½ handful of coriander, freshly chopped

2 teaspoons ground coriander

½ teaspoon baking powder

4 soft oval rolls

a handful of salad leaves

2 tomatoes, diced

salt and black pepper

sunflower oil, for shallow frying

Yoghurt sauce

125 g Greek-style yoghurt

1 tablespoon tahini (sesame seed paste)

1 garlic clove, crushed

½ tablespoon lemon juice

1 tablespoon olive oil

Falafels are Egyptian bean patties traditionally served in pita bread with salad leaves and hoummus. Here they make a great burger filling with a yoghurt dressing. You will need to use dried chickpeas and soak them overnight before starting the burgers (although you could cheat and use tinned chickpeas instead). You will also need a blender or food processor for this recipe.

Put the dried chickpeas in a bowl and add cold water to cover by a good 12 cm. Leave to soak overnight.

The next day, drain the chickpeas well, transfer to a blender or food processor and blend until coarsely ground. Add the onion, garlic, parsley, fresh and ground coriander, baking powder and some salt and pepper and blend until very smooth. Transfer to a bowl, cover and refrigerate for 30 minutes.

To make the yoghurt sauce, put the yoghurt, tahini, garlic, lemon juice and olive oil in a bowl and whisk until smooth. Season to taste with salt and pepper and set aside until required.

Using wet hands, shape the chickpea mixture into 8 medium patties. Heat a shallow layer of oil in a frying pan, add the patties and fry for 3 minutes on each side until golden and cooked through. Drain on kitchen paper.

Cut the rolls in half and fill with 2 patties, yoghurt sauce, salad leaves and diced tomato. Serve hot.

chunky aubergine burgers

chunky *aubergine* burgers

The smoky taste of char-grilled aubergines and the basil pesto give these burgers a distinctive Mediterranean flavour. You could replace the sliced tomatoes with semi-dried tomatoes if you like.

makes 4

Q

1 large aubergine, about 750 g

4 tablespoons olive oil

1 tablespoon balsamic vinegar

1 garlic clove, crushed

4 soft bread rolls, halved

2 beef tomatoes, thickly sliced

200 g mozzarella, sliced

a handful of rocket

salt and black pepper

pesto, to serve

Preheat the grill to high.

Cut the aubergine into 1-cm slices. Put the oil, vinegar, garlic and some salt and pepper in a bowl. Whisk to mix, then brush over the aubergine slices. Arrange them on a grill pan or in a baking dish and grill for 3–4 minutes on each side until charred and softened.

Lightly toast the rolls and top with a slice of aubergine. Spread with pesto, add another slice of aubergine, then add a slice of tomato and mozzarella. Drizzle with more pesto, then top with a few rocket leaves. Put the tops on the rolls and serve hot.

curried *sweet potato* burgers

You can either add some lime pickle and natural yoghurt to these nutty burgers or serve them rolled in warm chapatti bread. Be aware that you will need to refrigerate the burgers for 30 minutes before cooking.

makes 4

75 g bulghur wheat

400 g sweet potatoes, cubed

1½ tablespoons olive oil, plus extra for shallow frying

1 small onion, finely chopped

1 garlic clove, crushed

1 tablespoon curry powder

75 g blanched almonds, finely chopped

2 tablespoons freshly chopped coriander

1 egg, lightly beaten

4 tablespoons plain flour

4 burger buns

a handful of salad leaves

about 5 cm cucumber, sliced

4 tablespoons mango chutney

salt and black pepper

Put the bulghur wheat in a heatproof bowl, add boiling water to cover by 3 cm and set aside to soak for 20 minutes until tender. Drain well.

Meanwhile, steam the potatoes for 10–15 minutes until cooked. Drain well and mash with a potato masher. Heat the olive oil in a frying pan and fry the onion, garlic and curry powder for 10 minutes until the onion is softened.

Put the bulghur wheat, mashed potato, onion mixture, almonds, coriander, egg, flour and some salt and pepper in a bowl. Work together with your hands until evenly mixed. Cover and refrigerate for 30 minutes. Using wet hands, divide the mixture into 8 portions and shape into patties.

Heat a shallow layer of olive oil in a frying pan, add the patties and fry gently for 3–4 minutes on each side until golden and heated through. Cut the buns in half, toast and fill with 2 patties, salad leaves, cucumber slices and mango chutney. Serve hot.

greek omelette

olive oil, for frying

100 g cherry tomatoes, halved

4–5 bottled marinated peppers (hot ones, if you like them!)

3 spring onions, sliced

40 g stoned black olives, sliced

100 g feta

a small handful of parsley, freshly chopped

6 large eggs

salt and black pepper

Salad

200 g mixed leaves

1 tablespoon lemon juice

4 tablespoons olive oil

This is not a traditional recipe. It's been named a 'Greek omelette' simply because it contains Greek-inspired ingredients, many of which can probably be found at your local greengrocer shop. This omelette is fast to make, nice to look at and easy to eat, so you might find yourself cooking it often. Serve it hot or cold, with crusty bread or pita. The recipe serves 2 as a main course or 4 as a snack or starter.

Preheat the oven to 200°C (400°F) Gas 6.

Drizzle a little oil into a large, round, ovenproof dish. Arrange the tomatoes, peppers, spring onions and olives equally around the dish. Crumble in the feta, then grind black pepper over the top. Sprinkle with parsley.

Put the eggs in a separate bowl, beat well and season with a good pinch of salt. Pour over the ingredients in the dish. Bake in the preheated oven until puffed and just golden around the edges, 15–20 minutes.

To make the salad, put the leaves in a bowl, add the lemon juice, oil and some salt and pepper. Toss well, taste and adjust the seasoning with more salt and pepper if necessary. Serve with the omelette cut into wedges – hot, warm or at room temperature.

sweet potato and *brie* tortilla

Buy deep orange sweet potatoes to achieve the best effect for this colourful tortilla. To melt the Brie, the tortilla is finished in the oven, so use a pan with a heatproof handle.

serves 2–3

2 medium sweet potatoes, about 500 g, cut into chunks

4 tablespoons olive or sunflower oil

1 onion, halved lengthways and cut into 5-mm slices

5 large eggs

1 garlic clove, crushed

125 g Brie

salt and black pepper

Preheat the oven to 200°C (400°F) Gas 6.

Put the potatoes and 2 tablespoons of the oil in a roasting tin and toss to coat. Roast in the preheated oven for 15 minutes, then add the onion and mix well. Roast in the oven for a further 20 minutes, or until the potatoes and onion are tender.

Break the eggs into a large bowl and whisk briefly with a fork. Stir in the garlic and some salt and pepper. Add the cooked potatoes and onions and mix gently.

Heat the remaining oil in a small frying pan. Pour the tortilla mixture into the pan and cook over medium-low heat for 6–8 minutes, or until it has set around the edges and is lightly browned underneath.

Slice the Brie and arrange on top of the tortilla. Transfer the pan to the preheated oven for 5 minutes, or until the Brie has melted and the top of the tortilla has set. Serve hot or warm, cut into wedges.

roasted *vegetable* tortilla

1 red onion, cut into wedges

1 red pepper, deseeded and cut into thick strips

1 leek, thickly sliced

125 g butternut squash, peeled, deseeded and cubed

6 sprigs of thyme

2 garlic cloves, unpeeled

3 tablespoons olive or sunflower oil

6 large eggs

salt and black pepper

serves 3–4

There is nothing quite like the char-grilled flavour of roasted vegetables; as a tortilla filling they make a delicious alternative to the more traditional potato. You can roast the vegetables up to 24 hours in advance and keep chilled until you are ready to make the tortilla, but allow a little extra time to cook the tortilla because the vegetables will be cold. The tortilla is finished under the grill so use a pan with a heatproof handle.

Preheat the oven to 200°C (400°F) Gas 6.

Put the onion, red pepper, leek and squash in large roasting tin. Sprinkle with thyme and some salt and pepper. Bury the garlic cloves under the vegetables and sprinkle with 2 tablespoons of the oil. Roast in the preheated oven for 20 minutes. Turn the vegetables over and roast in the oven for a further 10 minutes.

Remove from the oven and leave to cool for 5 minutes. Remove the soft flesh from the roasted garlic and discard the skins. Discard the thyme stalks, removing any leaves still attached.

Break the eggs into a large bowl, add some salt and pepper and whisk briefly with a fork. Add the vegetables and mix gently.

Heat the remaining oil in a medium frying pan. Add the tortilla mixture and cook over medium-low heat for about 10 minutes or until the bottom is golden brown and the top almost set.

Slide under a preheated grill to finish cooking or put a plate over the top of the pan and invert so the tortilla falls onto the plate. Slide back into the pan and cook for 2–3 minutes. Leave to stand for 5 minutes to settle. Serve hot or at room temperature, cut into wedges.

courgette, potato and *onion* tortilla

550 g potatoes, cut horizontally into 5-mm slices

2 tablespoons olive oil

2 onions, halved lengthways and cut into 5-mm slices

2 courgettes, diced

6 large eggs

salt and black pepper

serves 4–6

This light lunch or supper ticks all the right boxes. It contains everyday ingredients, is simple to make and combines a balanced combination of protein and carbohydrates. Serve with a watercress and tomato salad and crusty bread. The tortilla is finished under the grill so use a pan with a heatproof handle.

Cook the potatoes in boiling salted water for about 6 minutes until tender. Drain in a colander and cool under cold running water, then set aside.

Heat 1 tablespoon of the oil in a large frying pan over medium-low heat. Add the onions and sauté, covered, for 10 minutes, stirring frequently, until softened but not browned. Add the courgettes and fry for another 3 minutes.

Meanwhile, lightly beat the eggs in a large bowl and season to taste. Add the cooked onions, courgettes and potatoes and turn until the vegetables are well coated in the eggs.

Heat the remaining oil in the frying pan. Remove the pan from the heat and carefully pour the egg mixture into it. Make sure the vegetables are evenly distributed in the pan, pressing them down into the egg.

Preheat the grill to medium.

Return the pan to the hob and cook the tortilla for 6 minutes, until the bottom is set and slightly golden. To cook the top of the tortilla, slide the pan under the grill and cook gently for 6–7 minutes, or until the egg is cooked. Alternatively, put a plate over the top of the pan and invert so the tortilla falls onto the plate. Slide back into the pan and cook for 2–3 minutes.

Allow the tortilla to cool slightly before cutting into wedges.

asian-style *tofu* omelette

This omelette has a distinctly Asian feel, with creamy cubes of tofu replacing the more traditional cheese.

serves
4

Q

Put the oil in a large frying pan with a heatproof handle over high heat. Add the shallots, broccoli and mushrooms and stir-fry for 3–4 minutes, until the mushrooms are soft and the broccoli turns bright green. Add the spinach and cook until just wilted. Add the soy sauce and stir. Arrange the tofu evenly over the vegetables.

Preheat the grill to high.

Meanwhile, lightly beat the eggs and season to taste. Pour into the pan and cook over high heat until the edges puffed. Place the pan under the grill and cook until golden and firm on top. Leave to cool a little before serving.

1 tablespoon olive oil

2 shallots, sliced

250 g tenderstem broccoli, chopped into small pieces

200 g shiitake mushrooms

50 g baby spinach leaves

2 teaspoons light soy sauce

300 g firm tofu, cubed

8 eggs

salt and white or black pepper

broccoli and potato frittata

The frittata is Italy's version of a flat, open-faced omelette. Ideally it should be cooked slowly, only lightly coloured and still slightly moist when served. Try to find really small waxy potatoes for this frittata – they are creamy and yellow and sweeter than most larger varieties, and particularly good with tenderstem broccoli. Tenderstem broccoli is part broccoli and part Chinese chard and can be added to stir-fries, pastas and salads. The frittata is finished under the grill so use a pan with a heatproof handle.

serves
4

8 small waxy potatoes, (such as Kipfler), quartered

250 ml vegetable stock

60 ml olive oil

250 g tenderstem broccoli, trimmed and halved lengthways

1 red onion, thinly sliced

8 eggs

100 g Parmesan, grated

mixed leaf salad, to serve

Put the potatoes in a large frying pan and pour over the stock. Put the pan over high heat and bring the stock to the boil. Boil for 10 minutes, turning the potatoes often, until almost all the stock has been absorbed.

Add the olive oil, broccoli and onion to the pan and cook for 1 minute, turning the vegetables to coat in the oil. Cover and cook for 2–3 minutes, to soften the broccoli.

Preheat the grill to high.

Lightly beat the eggs with half of the Parmesan and pour over the vegetables. Cover the pan and cook over medium heat for 8–10 minutes, until the eggs look set.

Sprinkle over the remaining cheese, then place under the grill and cook until the top of the frittata is golden. Alternatively, put a plate over the top of the pan and invert so the frittata falls onto the plate. Slide back into the pan and cook for 2–3 minutes.

Leave to cool slightly before removing from the pan. Cut into wedges and serve with a mixed leaf salad.

feta, tomato and *herb* omelette

serves
2

Q

You'll be surprised how tasty this omelette is, given how basic the ingredients and method are. It's really a simpler version of the Greek Omelette on page 160. All the flavour derives from the quality of the ingredients so if you can, buy your cherry tomatoes still on the vine – they taste so much better that way. This is the kind of recipe you want to have on standby when there are just two of you for dinner and you don't want to slave over anything too filling or complicated. The omelette is finished under the grill so use a pan with a heatproof handle.

5 large eggs

2 tablespoons freshly chopped basil

1 tablespoon freshly chopped mint

3 spring onions, finely chopped

2 tablespoons sunflower oil

75 g feta, crumbled

8 cherry tomatoes, halved

salt and black pepper

Break the eggs into a bowl and whisk briefly with a fork. Season with salt and pepper, add 2 tablespoons water, the basil, mint and spring onions and mix briefly.

Heat the oil in a small frying pan. Pour in the egg mixture and cook over medium heat for 4–5 minutes, drawing the mixture from the sides to the centre until the omelette is half cooked.

Preheat the grill to medium.

Top with the feta and the tomato halves, cut side up, and cook for 2 minutes. Slide under the grill and cook until light golden brown. Alternatively, put a plate over the top of the pan and invert so the omelette falls onto the plate. Slide back into the pan and cook for 2–3 minutes.

Slide onto a warmed plate and serve immediately.

easy speedy pizza

You can make your own pizza from scratch in half an hour. You can add anything you like as a topping – though this mixture is always popular.

makes 4

Preheat the oven to 200°C (400°F) Gas 6.

Sift the flour, sugar, bicarbonate of soda and salt into a large bowl. Stir in the dried herbs.

With your hand, make a hollow in the middle of the flour and pour in the buttermilk or the yoghurt and milk mixture. Using one hand, start to mix the flour into the liquid, then gradually work all the flour into the mixture to make a soft and slightly sticky dough. If there are dry crumbs and it is hard to work all the flour into the dough, add 1 tablespoon of buttermilk or milk. If the dough is sticky and feels very wet, work in a little more flour.

When the dough comes together in a ball, tip it out of the bowl onto a work surface lightly sprinkled with flour. Work the ball of dough with both hands for 1 minute until it looks smooth.

Divide the dough into 4 equal pieces. Shape each piece into a neat ball. Flour your hands, then gently pat out each piece of the dough to a circle about 17 cm across. Set the circles slightly apart on the greased trays.

To make the topping, put the chopped tomatoes in a bowl with the tomato purée, olive oil, herbs, garlic and some salt and pepper. Mix well.

Spoon 2 tablespoons of the tomato topping in the middle of each pizza base. Spread over the pizza, leaving a 2-cm border of uncovered dough all around the edge. Arrange the mozzarella over the topping. Finally, top with as many extras as you like.

Bake the pizzas in the preheated oven until light golden and bubbling – about 15–18 minutes.

Leave to cool for a couple of minutes before serving.

450 g plain flour, plus extra for dusting

1 teaspoon caster sugar

1 teaspoon bicarbonate of soda

1 teaspoon salt

½ teaspoon dried oregano or thyme

350 ml buttermilk or 175 ml natural yoghurt plus 175 ml milk

Topping

400-g tin chopped tomatoes

1 tablespoon tomato purée

1 tablespoon olive oil

1 teaspoon dried oregano or thyme

1 garlic clove, crushed

2 mozzarella balls, about 150 g each, sliced

salt and black pepper

Optional extras

green or black stoned olives, sliced red or green pepper or mushrooms

2 large baking trays, greased

food to impress

couscous with roast *squash, halloumi, dates* and *pistachios*

It might sound unusual, but peppermint tea is great for fluffing up the grains of couscous and works well alongside the sweetness of squash and salty, squeaky halloumi. It is strong and minty, so it only needs a brief stint in hot water.

serves
4–6

400 g butternut squash or pumpkin, peeled, deseeded and cut into wedges

3 tablespoons olive oil

3 dried bay leaves

3 sprigs of thyme

4 garlic cloves, unpeeled

2 large dried chillies or 1 teaspoon dried chilli flakes

250 g halloumi, cubed

25 g pistachios, shelled and chopped

2 peppermint tea bags

300 ml just-boiled water

200 g couscous

125 g fresh dates, stoned and finely chopped

salt and black pepper

Preheat the oven to 200°C (400°F) Gas 6.

Put the squash in a roasting tin, drizzle with 2 tablespoons of the olive oil and tuck in the bay leaves, thyme, garlic cloves and chillies or chilli flakes. Roast in the preheated oven for 25 minutes, or until the squash is almost tender. Raise the oven temperature to 240°C (475°F) Gas 9. Add the halloumi and pistachios, drizzle with the remaining olive oil and roast for a further 10 minutes, or until the halloumi is golden.

Meanwhile, put the peppermint tea bags in a heatproof jug or a teapot and pour over the hot water. Leave to steep for 1 minute, then discard the tea bags. Put the couscous and dates in a large bowl, season to taste and pour over the hot tea. Cover with clingfilm and leave for 5 minutes, or until the grains have swollen and absorbed all the tea.

Fluff up the couscous with a fork, stirring in about half the ingredients from the roasting tin at the same time, but leaving behind the whole chillies, if using. Spoon into 4–6 bowls and top with the remaining ingredients.

braised *fennel* with *polenta*

2 large fennel bulbs

65 ml olive oil

1 onion, chopped

2 garlic cloves, chopped

1 small red chilli, deseeded and chopped

a handful of parsley, freshly chopped

2 tablespoons lemon juice

2 tablespoons white wine

500 ml vegetable stock

a handful of small, stoned black olives

Polenta

500 ml milk

1 litre vegetable stock

200 g instant polenta

50 g butter

100 g Pecorino or Parmesan, grated

Try to buy fennel with the feathery leaves intact, as these can be added to the final stages of a dish or used as a garnish. While smaller, tender bulbs can be eaten raw, the larger, tougher ones are perfect when braised, as here. The polenta – made creamy with milk, butter and cheese – makes everything more filling and even tastier.

Cut about ½ cm from the gnarly stem on the bottom of the fennel bulbs. Cut off the fronds (the feathery leaves), chop finely and reserve. Cut off and discard all but about 1 cm from the dark green stems. Thinly slice the remaining white fennel bulb lengthways.

Put the oil in a heavy-based saucepan and set over high heat. Add the onions, garlic and chilli and cook for 2–3 minutes until softened. Add the parsley and fennel bulb and fronds and cook for 2–3 minutes, stirring often so that the fennel becomes coated in the oil. Add the lemon juice, wine and stock and bring to the boil. Cover with a lid and turn the heat down to a low simmer for 20 minutes, stirring occasionally. Add the olives, remove the lid and boil rapidly until there is only a little liquid left and the fennel is very soft and tender.

Meanwhile, to make the polenta, put the milk and stock in a saucepan and bring to a gentle simmer over medium heat. Slowly pour in the polenta in a steady stream and beat with a whisk until smooth. Reduce the heat to low and continue to beat for 2–3 minutes. When the mixture thickens, discard the whisk and use a wooden spoon. Add the butter and cheese and stir until melted into the polenta. Spoon some polenta onto serving plates, top with the braised fennel and serve.

feta-stuffed peppers

feta-stuffed *peppers*

This healthy combination of bulghur wheat, sharp feta and sweet peppers tastes divine.

serves
4

Put the bulghur wheat in a bowl, cover with boiling water and leave to stand for 30 minutes, until the grains are puffed and swollen. Drain, if necessary, and fluff with a fork to separate the grains.

Preheat the oven to 180°C (350°F) Gas 4.

Meanwhile, cut the peppers in half lengthways and scrape out and discard the seeds and membranes. Leave the stalks intact so the peppers hold their shape. Transfer the peppers to an ovenproof dish.

Put the apple and lemon juice in a bowl and mix lightly. Add the drained bulghur wheat, feta, herbs, garlic, ginger, raisins, spring onions and oil. Season with salt and pepper and mix well. Divide the mixture between the halved peppers. Pour a little water in the dish around the peppers and cook in the preheated oven for 20–25 minutes, until the filling is piping hot.

100 g bulghur wheat

2 yellow peppers

2 orange peppers

1 red apple, cored and chopped

1 tablespoon lemon juice

150 g feta, crumbled

3 tablespoons freshly chopped mixed herbs, such as dill, basil, parsley, mint and coriander

2 garlic cloves, crushed

3 cm fresh ginger, peeled and finely grated

50 g raisins

8 spring onions, chopped

1–2 tablespoons olive oil

salt and black pepper

baked *goats' cheese* on *toast*

Sometimes, only cheese on toast will do. But take some goats' cheese and a couple of slices of really good bread, and you have the most decadent and moreish cheese on toast imaginable.

serves
2

Q

Preheat the oven to 200°C (400°F) Gas 6.

Put the goats' cheese slices onto the prepared baking tray, sprinkle with a little oil, dot with thyme leaves and season with pepper. Bake in the preheated oven for 10–12 minutes until just starting to ooze and run.

Meanwhile, toast the bread and rub it with the garlic. When the cheese is ready, spread it onto the toasted bread and serve with a green salad.

4 thick slices of goats' cheese with rind, 50 g per serving

1 tablespoon freshly chopped thyme

4 slices of bread, preferably sourdough

1 garlic clove, halved

green salad, to serve

black pepper

olive oil, for sprinkling

a baking tray, lined with foil

baked *spinach* mornay

40 g butter

2 tablespoons plain flour

750 ml milk

200 g Fontina (or a similar cheese, like Gruyère or Edam), cubed

1 onion, chopped

1 garlic clove, chopped

1 kg spinach leaves, chopped

½ teaspoon grated nutmeg

toasted and buttered bread, to serve (optional)

serves 6

This is really rich and ideally served with something doughy like the Upside-down Tomato Tart on page 205 or a simple green salad with a tangy vinaigrette. It is also a great brunch dish, perfect with poached eggs and hot buttered toast.

Preheat oven to 180°C (350°F) Gas 4.

Put 25 g of the butter in a saucepan over medium heat. When it is melted and sizzling, add the flour and cook for 1 minute, stirring constantly, until a thick paste forms.

Reduce the heat to low and slowly pour the milk into the pan, whisking constantly, until all the milk is incorporated and the mixture is smooth and lump-free. Add the cheese and stir until it has melted into the sauce. Set aside until needed.

Heat the remaining butter in a large frying pan over high heat, add the onion and garlic and cook for 2–3 minutes, until the onion has softened. Add the spinach, cover with a lid, and cook for 4–5 minutes, stirring often, until the spinach has wilted. Transfer the spinach to a large bowl. Pour in the cheese sauce and stir to combine.

Spoon the mixture into a large baking dish. Sprinkle the nutmeg over the top and bake in the preheated oven for 30 minutes until the top of the mornay is golden and bubbling. Serve on slices of toasted and buttered bread if you like.

aubergine, tomato and *parmesan* gratin

serves
4

A gratin is usually a shallow dish of vegetables topped with breadcrumbs or grated cheese and baked in the oven. This one is particularly pretty and bursting with flavour. Tomato halves are baked with briefly fried, sliced aubergines and Parmesan.

1 large aubergine

500 g very ripe tomatoes

about 150 ml olive oil

4 tablespoons freshly chopped basil

125 g Parmesan, grated

salt and black pepper

a shallow ovenproof dish, well greased

Cut the aubergine lengthways into 5-mm slices. Sprinkle with salt and leave to drain in a colander for 30 minutes. Rinse well and pat dry with kitchen paper. Cut the tomatoes in half through the middle.

Preheat the oven to 200°C (400°F) Gas 6.

Heat the oil in a large frying pan and fry the aubergines in batches until deep golden brown. Drain on kitchen paper. Arrange a layer of aubergines in the prepared dish, then top with a layer of tomato halves, cut side up. Sprinkle with the chopped basil, salt, pepper and half the Parmesan. Add another layer of aubergines, then sprinkle with the remaining Parmesan.

Bake in the preheated oven for 20–25 minutes, or until browned and bubbling on top. Leave to cool slightly and serve warm, or cool completely and serve as a salad.

mixed *vegetable* tian

A tian is a shallow baking dish, often glazed earthenware. Like the word 'casserole', the name has also come to mean the food cooked in it. These days tians usually contain vegetables and herbs and sometimes cheese and eggs. This is a delicious version that can be served in spoonfuls or in wedges, with bread or a leafy side salad.

Put the aubergine in a colander, sprinkle with the salt and set aside for 15 minutes or until all the other ingredients have been prepared.

Preheat the oven to 200°C (400°F) Gas 6.

Heat the oil and 1 tablespoon of the butter in a large frying pan, add the garlic, onion, spring onions, spinach and beans and sauté over medium heat for 6–8 minutes, stirring constantly, until the vegetables are soft but still colourful. Remove with a slotted spoon.

Pat the aubergine dry with kitchen paper, removing most of the salt. Add the remaining butter to the frying pan, add the aubergine and sauté for 5 minutes.

Put the eggs, crème fraîche and Parmesan in a bowl and whisk with a fork.

Transfer the aubergine, vegetables and their juices and oil into a shallow baking dish, distributing them evenly. Pour the egg and cheese mixture over the top and bake in the preheated oven for 5 minutes. Reduce the heat to 180°C (350°F) Gas 4 for a further 20 minutes and cook until set and nicely browned.

serves
4

1 small aubergine, cubed

2 teaspoons salt

2 tablespoons olive oil

2 tablespoons butter

4 garlic cloves, chopped

1 onion, sliced

4 spring onions, sliced

a handful of spinach or Swiss chard, chopped

a handful of green beans, cut into 3-cm lengths

8 eggs

250 ml crème fraîche or soured cream

75 g Parmesan, Pecorino, or Gruyère, grated

pumpkin and *gorgonzola* risotto

500 g pumpkin, peeled, deseeded and cubed

1 tablespoon olive oil

1 litre vegetable stock

2 tablespoons butter

1 leek, halved lengthways and thinly sliced

1 garlic clove, chopped

330 g risotto rice

50 g Gorgonzola, crumbled

serves
4

This is similar to the Roasted Butternut Squash Risotto on page 135, but richer and altogether more special with the addition of luxuriously creamy Gorgonzola. It's also better for guests because the recipe serves 4 rather than 2. Make this in the autumn when pumpkins are in season.

Preheat the oven to 180°C (350°F) Gas 4.

Put the pumpkin in a roasting tin, drizzle with the olive oil and roast in the preheated oven for 30 minutes.

While the pumpkin is cooking in the oven, make the risotto. Put the stock in a saucepan. Heat until almost boiling, then reduce the heat until barely simmering to keep it hot.

Melt the butter in a large saucepan over high heat and add the leek and garlic. Cook for 4–5 minutes, stirring often, until the leeks have just softened.

Add the rice to the leeks and stir for 1 minute, until the rice is well coated with oil. Add a ladle of the hot stock to the rice and cook, stirring constantly, until the rice has absorbed most of the liquid. Repeat this process until all the liquid has been absorbed and the rice is tender but still firm (al dente), about 20–25 minutes.

Add the roasted pumpkin pieces. Remove the pan from the heat, stir in the Gorgonzola and serve immediately.

fennel and *lemon* risotto

Fennel is a bit of an acquired taste, since it has a distinctive, aniseed-like flavour that's not to everyone's liking. If you do like it, and your friends are just as willing to eat it, make this light, basic risotto that will have everyone asking for more.

serves
4

2 fennel bulbs

900 ml vegetable stock

50 g unsalted butter

1 tablespoon olive oil

8 shallots, finely chopped

grated zest of 2 lemons

275 g risotto rice

75 ml white wine

100 g Parmesan, grated

2 tablespoons single cream

salt and black pepper

Cut about ½ cm from the gnarly stem on the bottom of the fennel bulbs. Cut off the fronds (the feathery leaves) and reserve. Cut off and discard all but about 1 cm from the dark green stems. Thinly slice the remaining white fennel bulb.

Put the stock in a saucepan. Heat until almost boiling, then reduce the heat until barely simmering to keep it hot.

Heat the butter and oil in a large saucepan over medium heat. Add the shallots and cook for 1–2 minutes, until softened but not browned. Add the fennel and lemon zest.

Add the rice and stir until the grains are well coated and glistening, about 1 minute. Pour in the wine and stir until it has been completely absorbed.

Add 1 ladle of hot stock and simmer, stirring until it has been absorbed. Continue to add the stock at intervals and cook as before, until the liquid has been absorbed and the rice is tender but still firm (al dente), about 18–20 minutes. Reserve the last ladle of stock.

Add the reserved stock, Parmesan, cream and some salt and pepper. Mix well. Remove from the heat, cover and leave to rest for 2 minutes. Spoon into bowls, top with the reserved fennel fronds and serve.

risotto with *aubergine, pine nuts* and *tomatoes*

1 small aubergine, about 200 g, diced

50 g pine nuts

3 tablespoons olive oil

4–6 firm tomatoes, deseeded and chopped

900 ml vegetable stock

50 g unsalted butter

8 shallots, finely chopped

2 garlic cloves, crushed

275 g risotto rice

1 glass of white wine, about 125 ml

100 g Parmesan, grated

a handful of parsley, freshly chopped

a handful of basil, freshly chopped

salt and black pepper

serves 4

There are several steps to this risotto, but they all help to make the finished dish extra delicious. Salting the aubergines before cooking will remove any bitterness and toasting the pine nuts until golden will intensify their nutty flavour. This is really a complete main course in one, with vegetables thrown in, so you probably won't need anything on the side.

Put the aubergine in a colander set over a bowl. Sprinkle with salt and leave to stand for 10–15 minutes.

Meanwhile, heat a frying pan over medium heat and drop in the pine nuts. Toast them, stirring frequently, until golden. Watch them carefully as they burn easily.

Rinse the aubergine to remove the salt and pat dry with kitchen paper. Heat 2 tablespoons of the oil in a frying pan, add the aubergine and cook until golden. Add the tomatoes and cook until softened.

Put the stock in a saucepan. Heat until almost boiling, then reduce the heat until barely simmering to keep it hot.

Heat the butter and remaining oil in a large saucepan over medium heat. Add the shallots and cook for 1–2 minutes, until softened but not browned. Add the garlic.

Add the rice and stir until the grains are well coated and glistening, about 1 minute. Pour in the wine and stir until it has been completely absorbed.

Add 1 ladle of hot stock and simmer, stirring until it has been absorbed. Continue to add the stock at intervals and cook as before, until the liquid has been absorbed and the rice is tender but firm (al dente), about 18–20 minutes. Reserve the last ladle of stock.

Add the reserved stock, the aubergine and tomato mixture, the Parmesan, pine nuts, parsley, basil and some salt and pepper. Mix well. Remove from the heat, cover and leave to rest for 2 minutes before serving.

*aubergine and
tomato stacks*

aubergine and *tomato* stacks

This is a smart and filling dish, with bubbly, molten cheese. Taleggio cheese is full of nuttiness when melted, but you could also use Gruyère or mozzarella. Beef tomatoes are perfect here as they are large, great to slice and easy to stack.

serves
4

1 aubergine, about 250 g, sliced into 12 thick rounds

1 large beef tomato, about 150 g, sliced into 8 rounds

250 g Taleggio, or any other good melting cheese, cut into 8 slices

olive oil, for sprinkling

dried chilli flakes, for sprinkling (optional)

Preheat the oven to 190°C (375°F) Gas 5.

Lightly brush a frying pan with oil. Working in batches, add the aubergine slices and cook for a few minutes on each side until browned and softening.

To make the stacks, arrange 4 slices of aubergine apart in an oiled baking dish. Add 1 slice of tomato to each one, then 1 slice of cheese. Repeat until each stack has 3 slices of aubergine, 2 of tomato and 3 of cheese, ending with aubergine. Sprinkle each stack with olive oil and chilli flakes, if using.

Bake in the preheated oven for about 15 minutes until soft, bubbly and golden. Serve hot with a crisp green salad or lightly steamed vegetables.

pumpkin and *feta* parcels

These are based on Argentinian empañadas, which are often filled with spiced meat, but this is a great vegetarian version.

makes
12

500 g pumpkin, peeled, deseeded and chopped

1 red onion, chopped

2 garlic cloves, crushed

½ teaspoon cumin seeds

2 tablespoons olive oil

2 teaspoons white wine vinegar

3 sheets of ready-rolled puff pastry, defrosted if frozen

60 g feta, grated

1 tablespoon milk

a baking tray, lined with greaseproof paper

a biscuit cutter, about 12 cm in diameter

Preheat the oven to 220°C (425°F) Gas 7.

Combine the pumpkin, onion, garlic, cumin and oil in a small baking dish. Add the vinegar and 65 ml water and cook in the oven for about 30 minutes, until the pumpkin is tender and golden and the liquid has evaporated. Transfer to a bowl (and leave the oven on), roughly mash with a fork and season to taste. Set aside to cool.

Unroll the pastry and lay it on a clean work surface. Use the biscuit cutter to stamp out 12 circles. Put 1 tablespoon of filling in the centre of each circle and top with a little crumbled feta. Brush cold water around the edge of each one just to moisten and fold over to form a half-moon shape. Pinch the edges between your thumb and index finger to seal. Put on the prepared baking tray. Brush the top of each with milk. Bake in the preheated oven for about 20 minutes, until lightly golden. Serve warm.

courgette fritters

 makes 15

3 tablespoons olive oil, plus extra for frying

1 large onion, finely chopped

4 spring onions, including green parts, chopped

2 garlic cloves, crushed

600 g courgettes, trimmed and rinsed

2 small eggs

120 g breadcrumbs

4 tablespoons self-raising flour, plus 5–6 tablespoons, for rolling

200 g feta, crumbled

100 g Parmesan, Gruyère or Cheddar, grated

1 tablespoon dried oregano

1 tablespoon dried mint

black pepper

If you've never made fritters before, try these! They are a popular snack in homes and restaurants of the Greek island called Alonnisos. The recipe makes about 15 so it's a great one to turn to when you're feeding a few people. Serve them with a tomato and rocket salad.

Heat the olive oil in a frying pan, add the onion and spring onions and sauté gently until translucent, up to 20 minutes. Add the garlic, fry for 1 minute and remove from the heat. Leave to cool a little.

Grate the courgettes coarsely, put in a colander and set aside for about 30 minutes to allow the excess moisture to seep out.

Put the eggs in a bowl and beat lightly. Squeeze the courgettes with your hands to extract as much moisture as possible – this is very important! Add to the bowl, then add the onion mixture, the breadcrumbs, the 4 tablespoons flour, feta, Parmesan, oregano, mint and pepper. Mix with a fork. It should be dry enough to handle but, if not, add a little more flour.

Put a double sheet of greaseproof paper on a work surface and add the remaining flour. Take 1 tablespoon of the mixture, roll it in the flour, then make a round, flat shape with your hands, about 5 cm in diameter. The rounds are easier to handle when well coated in flour. Continue until the mixture is finished.

Heat some oil in a large, non-stick frying pan and fry the fritters, in batches, for about 3 minutes on each side until crisp and golden. Drain on kitchen paper before serving.

mushroom and pepper
tortilla

mushroom and *pepper* tortilla

This tortilla is designed to be served as tapas – a traditional Spanish snack – and it's made particularly easy here because it is cooked in the oven. If you want to make the tapas in advance, serve them cold or reheat for a few minutes in a medium oven.

serves
4

Preheat the oven to 200°C (400°F) Gas 6.

Pour 1 tablespoon of the oil into the cake tin and put in the preheated oven to heat.

Meanwhile, heat the remaining oil in a large frying pan, add the sliced potatoes and onion and cook over medium heat for about 15 minutes, turning occasionally, until almost tender. Add the mushrooms and pepper and cook for 5 minutes.

Break the eggs into a large bowl and whisk briefly with a fork. Add the oregano and season with salt and pepper. Remove the vegetables from the pan with a slotted spoon, add to the bowl of eggs and stir gently.

Transfer to the preheated cake tin, return to the oven and cook for about 15–20 minutes, or until the egg is just set in the centre. Leave to stand for 10 minutes, then serve warm, cut into small squares.

3 tablespoons olive or sunflower oil

2 potatoes, about 250 g, peeled and thinly sliced

1 small onion, halved and thinly sliced

75 g button mushrooms, sliced

1 orange pepper, deseeded and cut into strips

5 large eggs

1 teaspoon dried oregano

salt and black pepper

a 20-cm shallow, non-stick cake tin

char-grilled *pepper* frittata

serves 2-3

1 small red pepper, quartered and deseeded

1 small yellow pepper, quartered and deseeded

1 small green pepper, quartered and deseeded

2 tablespoons ricotta or mascarpone

6 large eggs

2 tablespoons freshly chopped thyme

2 tablespoons olive or sunflower oil

1 large red onion, sliced

1 tablespoon balsamic vinegar

2 garlic cloves, crushed

salt and black pepper

This is colourful, packed with peppers and perfect for preparing in advance. You can char-grill and peel the peppers the day before, if you like, then make the frittata itself on the morning that you're entertaining. It's delicious served hot or at room temperature. You can cut it into wedges or bars to serve as a starter, or if you're having a party, just double or triple the recipe, as necessary. The frittata is finished under the grill so use a pan with a heatproof handle.

Preheat the grill to hot.

Put the peppers, skin-side up, under the grill and cook until the skins have blackened. Transfer to a bowl, cover with a plate or clingfilm, and leave to cool. This will steam off the skins, making them easier to remove.

Put the ricotta or mascarpone in a large bowl, add 1 egg and mix to loosen the cheese. Whisk in the remaining eggs with a fork. Season with salt, pepper and thyme and stir into the cheese mixture.

Peel the blackened skins off the peppers and rinse under cold running water. Pat dry with kitchen paper and cut into thick strips. Stir into the bowl.

Heat half the oil in a small frying pan, add the sliced onion and balsamic vinegar and cook over gentle heat for about 10 minutes until softened. Add the garlic and cook for 1 minute.

Using a slotted spoon, add the onion to the egg mixture and stir. Add the remaining oil to the pan and heat gently. Pour the frittata mixture into the pan and cook over low heat until almost set, puffy and light golden brown on the underside.

Finish under a preheated grill or put a plate or flat saucepan lid on top of the pan and invert the pan so the frittata drops onto the plate or lid. Slide back into the pan and cook for 30–60 seconds. Transfer to a plate and serve hot or at room temperature, cut into wedges or bars.

asparagus, sweetcorn and *goats' cheese* frittata

Crunchy asparagus and sweetcorn work nicely here combined with eggs, creamy goats' cheese and fresh, tangy dill. You might think it's odd or annoying to use corn-on-the-cob for a frittata, but hopefully you will notice how much fresher and nicer it tastes than the frozen or tinned variety. Plus, of course, your guests will appreciate the extra effort! That said, if you need to save time or you can't find fresh cobs, use 250 g tinned or frozen (and thawed) sweetcorn instead. The frittata is finished under the grill so use a pan with a heatproof handle.

serves
4

2 bunches of thin asparagus spears

2 fresh corn-on-the-cobs

50 g butter

4 spring onions, finely chopped

a handful of dill, freshly chopped

8 eggs, beaten

200 g firm goats' cheese, broken into pieces

salt and black pepper

Trim or snap off the woody ends from the asparagus and cut the spears into 2–3-cm pieces. Shuck the corn kernels from the cobs by very carefully holding a cob upright and slicing off the corn by running a knife downwards. Mind your fingers!

Heat half of the butter in a large, non-stick frying pan over medium heat. Add the asparagus, sweetcorn and spring onions and fry for 2–3 minutes, stirring often. Transfer the vegetables to a large bowl and add the dill, reserving a little to use as garnish. Wipe the pan clean. Add the beaten eggs to the vegetables, gently stirring to combine, and season well with salt and pepper.

Preheat the grill to high.

Put the remaining butter in the pan and set over high heat. Swirl the pan around as the butter melts so that it coats the bottom and just starts to sizzle. Pour the frittata mixture into the pan and reduce the heat to medium. Arrange the pieces of goats' cheese over the top of the frittata and gently push them into the mixture. Cook for about 8 minutes, until the sides of the frittata start to puff up (reduce the heat if the bottom appears to be cooking too quickly).

Keep the frittata in the pan and place it under the preheated grill. Cook for 1 minute only just to set the top. Leave to cool a little in the pan, sprinkle with the reserved dill and serve immediately.

soufflé cheese omelette

soufflé *cheese* omelette

4 large eggs, separated

2 tomatoes, halved horizontally

a small knob of butter

50 g Cheddar, grated

salt and black pepper

serves
2

Q

This is the breakfast or brunch you want to make for a special someone. It's a soufflé-like omelette that's easy to whip up but looks like you've made a real effort. Serve it with the grilled tomato and some toast on the side and you're guaranteed to be in the good books. Don't forget to make some for yourself too!

Preheat the grill to medium. Line the grill pan with foil.

Meanwhile, whisk the egg whites in a large, clean bowl until they form stiff peaks. It will be much quicker if you do this with a handheld electric whisk. Season the egg yolks with salt and pepper and beat them in a separate bowl until even in colour and texture. Carefully fold the egg whites into the egg yolks using a metal spoon.

Put the tomatoes under the grill and cook for 6–8 minutes, turning once. After the tomato has been cooking for 4 minutes, heat the butter in a medium-sized non-stick frying pan. When the butter has melted, swirl it around the pan to cover the base.

Tip the egg mixture into the pan and flatten gently with a spatula until it covers the base of the pan. Cook over medium heat for 2 minutes, then sprinkle the cheese over the centre of the omelette. Cook for another minute, or until the base is light golden.

Carefully fold the omelette in half to cover the cheese. When the egg is set, slide onto a plate. Serve with the grilled tomato and some toast.

squash and *sage* frittata

There is something about the musty sharpness of sage that works so well with the sweetness of caramelized squash. Like other frittatas and tortillas, this is a very adaptable dish – cut into wedges and served with a green salad, it makes a great lunch. Cut into much smaller, bite-sized pieces, it works well as a nibble for a drinks party. Stuffed into a hollowed-out crusty loaf and drizzled with olive oil, it's even suitable for a picnic! The frittata is finished under the grill so use a pan with a heatproof handle (and a lid, for the first step).

serves
4

4 tablespoons olive oil

2 large onions, halved and thinly sliced

¼ teaspoon dried chilli flakes (or more to taste)

2 garlic cloves, halved

1 butternut squash (about 650 g), peeled, deseeded and cut into 1–2-cm dice

1 tablespoon freshly chopped sage

8 large eggs

2–3 tablespoons freshly chopped parsley

15 g butter

150 g firm goats' cheese, cut into 1-cm cubes

salt and black pepper

Heat the oil in a large frying pan over medium heat. Add the onions and 2 good pinches of salt. Stir, then cover and reduce the heat to low. Cook very gently, stirring occasionally, until the onions are meltingly soft and golden yellow, about 20 minutes.

Raise the heat slightly and add the chilli flakes, garlic and squash. Stir well. Cook gently, stirring frequently, until the squash is just tender, about 10 minutes. Discard the garlic. Fry the squash a little more until it starts to brown, then stir in the sage and cook for a few more minutes. Leave it to cool slightly.

Preheat the grill to medium.

In a bowl, whisk the eggs and beat in the parsley, then stir in the cooked squash and onions. Season with a little salt and black pepper.

Put the frying pan back over medium heat. Add the butter to the pan, and as it foams, pour in the egg and squash mixture and use a spatula to level it. Scatter the goats' cheese evenly over the top. Cook for about 5–6 minutes until the underside is golden brown and set. Put the frittata under the grill and cook until it is evenly browned, slightly puffed up and the egg is fully set. Serve warm or at room temperature.

roast *tomato, goats' cheese* and *rocket* tartlets

2 x 375-g packets of ready-rolled puff pastry, defrosted if frozen

2 tablespoons olive oil

2 tablespoons tomato purée

a handful of basil, freshly chopped

6 ripe tomatoes

100 g firm goats' cheese, crumbled

1 teaspoon caster sugar

40 g rocket or watercress

25 g Parmesan, shaved with a vegetable peeler

salt and black pepper

flour, for dusting

serves
4

Your guests will be delighted with these home-made tartlets. There's something about individual little tarts that looks so impressive and professional. The pastry can be cooked ahead of time and the topping added at the last moment. Ready-rolled puff pastry is a great help for cooks with little time to spare.

Preheat the oven to 220°C (425°F) Gas 7.

Lightly flour a work surface. Lay out the pastry and cut it into 4 x 15-cm rounds using a small plate as a guide. Prick all over vigorously with a fork and place on a baking tray. Cover with greaseproof paper, then put another baking tray on top. Bake in the preheated oven for about 15–20 minutes until golden brown. Cooking the pastry this way will ensure that it does not puff up too much but remains crisp. Remove from the oven and set aside.

Preheat the grill to high.

Mix together the olive oil, tomato purée and chopped basil. Spread this mixture over the cooked pastry rounds right to the edge.

If you have time, skin the tomatoes. To do this, follow the instructions under Ingredients Tips on page 10.

Slice the tomatoes finely and arrange them on top of the cooked pastry rounds, making sure they overlap and reach the edges, otherwise the pastry edges will burn. Scatter the goats' cheese over the top, season with salt and pepper and sprinkle over the caster sugar.

Put the tarts on a baking tray and place under the grill to cook until the cheese begins to melt and bubble. Transfer to plates and top each tart with rocket leaves or watercress and Parmesan shavings. Serve immediately.

Variation You can use other cheeses, such as crumbled feta, sliced mozzarella, cubed Roquefort or grated Cheddar.

upside-down *tomato* tart

This is a version of a tarte Tatin, a French tart essentially made upside-down on the hob to start with, then baked in the oven. The good news is that you need barely any ingredients, and you buy the pastry ready-made and ready-rolled so there's very little for you to do! This tart combines fresh rosemary and little capers but you could add any combination of ingredients that takes your fancy, such as olives, oregano or garlic. It serves 4 as a starter or 2 as a generous main course. This tart is finished in the oven so use a frying pan with a heatproof handle.

serves
2–4

2 tablespoons olive oil, plus extra for drizzling

2 teaspoons capers, rinsed if salted

10–12 fresh rosemary needles

3 ripe tomatoes, thickly sliced

375-g packet of ready-rolled puff pastry, defrosted if frozen

black pepper

Preheat the oven to 220°C (425°F) Gas 7.

Put the oil, capers and rosemary in a medium, non-stick frying pan. Put over high heat and when the capers start to sizzle add the tomatoes, firmly pressing them down in a single layer in the pan. Cook for 3–4 minutes to allow the tomatoes to sizzle and soften.

Place the sheet of pastry over the tomatoes, folding in the corners and being careful not to press down on the tomatoes. Transfer the pan to the preheated oven and cook for 18–20 minutes, until the pastry is puffed and golden. Remove the pan from the oven and let the tart rest for a couple of minutes.

Place a serving plate that is larger than the frying pan upside-down on top of the pan and quickly flip the pan over so the tart falls onto the plate. Sprinkle with black pepper and a drizzle of olive oil and cut into wedges.

tomato and *olive* tart with *parmesan*

375-g packet of ready-rolled puff pastry, defrosted if frozen

125 g red cherry tomatoes, halved

125 g yellow cherry tomatoes, halved

50 g semi-dried or sun-dried tomatoes, halved

50 g stoned black olives, halved

2 tablespoons olive oil

25 g Parmesan, shaved with a vegetable peeler

salt and black pepper

flour, for dusting

a handful of rocket leaves, to serve

serves
3–4

Q

The loveliest thing about this tart is its vibrant colours, so try to find yellow cherry tomatoes to complement the regular red ones. If you are lucky enough to have a market near you, you might find them there. Serve simply with rocket leaves.

Preheat the oven to 220°C (425°F) Gas 7.

Lightly flour a baking tray. Lay out the pastry and roll it or cut it as necessary to form a rectangle, about 25 x 30 cm. Using the blade of a sharp knife, gently tap the edges several times (this will help the pastry rise and the edges separate) and prick all over with a fork.

Put the tomatoes, olives, oil and some salt and pepper in a bowl and mix lightly. Spoon the mixture over the pastry. Bake in the preheated oven for about 12–15 minutes until risen and golden.

Remove from the oven and sprinkle with the Parmesan. Cut into 3 or 4 slices and serve hot with a handful of rocket leaves.

belgian *leek* tart

This tart is a little like a quiche – but for cheats! Use a shop-bought pastry case and all you have to do is make the filling. There is nothing quite like the combination of meltingly soft sweet leeks, cream and pastry.

serves
4–6

75 g butter

900 g leeks, thickly sliced

1 teaspoon salt

4 egg yolks

300 ml double cream or crème fraîche

grated nutmeg, to taste

a ready-made 20-cm shortcrust pastry case

salt and black pepper

Preheat the oven to 200°C (400°F) Gas 6.

Melt the butter in a large saucepan and add the leeks, stirring to coat. Add a few tablespoons of water and the 1 teaspoon salt, and cover with a lid. Steam very gently for at least 30 minutes (trying not to look too often!) until soft and melting. Remove the lid and cook for a few minutes to evaporate any excess liquid – the mixture should be quite thick. Leave to cool.

Put the egg yolks and cream or crème fraîche into a bowl, add salt, pepper and nutmeg to taste and beat well. Set the ready-made pastry case on a baking tray. Spoon the cooled leeks evenly into the pastry case, fluffing them up a bit with a fork. Pour the eggs and cream mixture over the top.

Bake in the preheated oven for 30 minutes or until set and pale golden brown. Serve warm.

desserts

juicy fruit crisp

juicy *fruit* crisp

Lovely at any time of year, this pudding is a combination of juicy fruits and a crunchy topping. Eat warm or cold with ice cream or yoghurt.

serves
4

2 large Granny Smith apples or 2 medium pears, peeled, cored and chopped

250 g fresh or frozen raspberries, blueberries or blackberries (no need to thaw)

2 tablespoons caster or Demerara sugar

Topping

125 g plain flour

80 g Demerara sugar

90 g unsalted butter, chilled and cubed

a medium baking dish, greased

Preheat the oven to 190°C (375°F) Gas 5.

Put the fruit in the dish, then add the berries. Sprinkle with the sugar and toss gently until just mixed. Spread the fruit evenly in the dish.

To make the topping, put the flour, sugar and butter in a mixing bowl. Using your fingertips, rub the mixture together until it becomes soft and sticky and there are pea-sized lumps of dough. Sprinkle this mixture over the fruit but don't press it down.

Bake in the preheated oven for 25 minutes until bubbling and golden on top. Serve the crisp hot, warm or cold.

pan *plum* crumble

This comforting crumble is cooked under the grill and you can even serve it at the table straight out of the frying pan – it doesn't get any more casual than that! The crumble is finished under the grill so use a frying pan with a heatproof handle.

serves
4–6

Q

185 ml orange juice

2 tablespoons caster sugar

6 ripe plums, halved and stoned

100 g self-raising flour

60 g soft brown sugar

60 g porridge oats

50 g unsalted butter, chilled and cubed

Put the orange juice and caster sugar in a small frying pan over high heat. Bring the mixture to the boil, then reduce the heat to medium. Add the plums, cut-side down, and cook for 5 minutes. Turn the plums over and cook for a further 5 minutes, until they have softened yet still retain their shape and the liquid has almost evaporated. Remove the pan from the heat and set aside.

Preheat the grill to medium.

Put the flour, brown sugar and oats in a bowl and mix just to combine. Add the butter and use your fingertips to rub it into the dry ingredients.

Sprinkle the mixture evenly over the plums and slide the frying pan under the grill for 2–3 minutes, until the crumble is golden. Serve warm.

nectarine and *pistachio* crumble

serves 6
Q

70 g shelled pistachio nuts, finely chopped

50 g ground almonds

60 g ground oatmeal

50 g unsalted butter, chilled and cubed

60 g plain flour

50 g soft brown sugar

6 nectarines

Crumbles are normally considered to be a comforting winter pudding, but this deliciously light, nutty version makes the most of juicy summer nectarines. It takes very little time to prepare and, like most crumbles, tastes sublime with ice cream.

Preheat the oven to 220°C (425°F) Gas 7.

Put the pistachio nuts, almonds, oatmeal and butter in a mixing bowl. Use your fingertips to rub the ingredients together until the mixture resembles coarse breadcrumbs. Add the flour and sugar and rub together to combine. At this stage, you can cover and refrigerate the topping until needed.

Line a baking tray with greaseproof paper. Cut the nectarines in half. If the stone does not come out easily, don't worry – simply slice the flesh off the fruit and drop it directly onto the baking tray. Sprinkle the crumble topping evenly over the nectarines and bake in the preheated oven for about 10–15 minutes, until the fruit is soft and juicy and the topping is a golden colour. Serve warm.

double *chocolate* fruity squares

makes 9

200 g dark chocolate

100 g sunflower margarine

2 tablespoons orange juice

150 g digestive biscuits

60 g white chocolate

50 g raisins

75 g dried apricots, chopped

50 g dried cherries or cranberries

a baking tin, 18 cm square, lightly greased

This is great! It's similar to refrigerator cake (so it doesn't need baking) but made with dried fruit, and margarine instead of butter, so it's a healthy option.

Break the dark chocolate into small squares and put them in a saucepan. Add the margarine and orange juice and heat very gently for 3–4 minutes, stirring occasionally, until melted. Stir until smooth.

Put the biscuits in a polythene bag and crush with a rolling pin. Roughly chop the white chocolate. Add the crushed biscuits, white chocolate and all the dried fruit to the melted chocolate mixture. Stir well.

Spoon the mixture into the prepared baking tin and press down lightly with the back of a wooden spoon. Transfer to the refrigerator and leave to set for at least 2 hours. Cut into squares to serve. Store lightly covered in the refrigerator for up to 4 days.

*nectarine and
pistachio crumble*

coconut creamed *rice* with poached *plums*

Tinned coconut milk is a useful ingredient to have in your kitchen cupboards, as it can be used in lots of dishes, both savoury and sweet. When you're buying the plums for this recipe, choose a sweet, large variety of plum and pick fruits with a silvery patina, as it's an indicator of freshness. The coconut creamed rice is also lovely with poached cherries.

serves
6

8 plums, halved and stoned

115 g light brown soft sugar

1 cinnamon stick

2 cardamom pods

Coconut creamed rice

100 g short-grain rice

2 x 400-ml tins coconut milk

115 g caster sugar

125 ml whipping cream

To make the coconut creamed rice, put the rice in a sieve and rinse it under cold running water until the water runs clear. Drain well. Put the rice in a large saucepan over high heat and add the coconut milk and sugar. Bring to a gentle boil, then reduce the heat to low and cook for 25–30 minutes, stirring often to ensure that the rice doesn't catch. Leave to cool. Whip the cream until soft peaks form, then fold it into the rice mixture.

Meanwhile, put the plums, sugar, cinnamon stick and cardamom pods in a saucepan and add 250 ml water. Bring to the boil, then reduce the heat to low and cook for 20 minutes, gently turning the plums often, until they soften but retain their shape. Remove the cinnamon stick and cardamom pods from the pan.

Divide the creamed rice between dishes and spoon the warm plums over the top. Serve immediately.

raspberry and *almond* tart

1 egg

3 tablespoons caster sugar

1 tablespoon plain flour,
plus extra for dusting

75 g unsalted butter

150 g raspberries, scattered
on a tray and frozen until firm

chilled cream, to serve
(optional)

Pastry

50 g ground almonds

200 g plain flour

80 g caster sugar

125 g unsalted butter, chilled
and cubed

a rectangular tart tin,
37 x 10 cm, lightly greased

 serves 6–8

This tart tastes better the day after it's made, which makes it ideal for preparing ahead of time. Be aware that you will need to freeze the raspberries before you start baking. This makes them firm enough to retain their shape while they're baking and stops them bleeding into the tart.

Preheat the oven to 180°C (350°F) Gas 4.

To make the pastry, put the ground almonds, flour and sugar in a mixing bowl. Add the butter and mix in with your fingertips until the mixture resembles coarse breadcrumbs. Add 2 tablespoons cold water and bring together until just combined.

Tip the pastry out onto a lightly floured work surface and knead to form a ball. Roll it out between 2 layers of greaseproof paper until it is about 5 cm longer and 5 cm wider than the tart tin. Carefully lift the pastry into the tin and use your fingers to press it down into the base and sides, letting it overhang. Prick the base all over with a fork and bake in the preheated oven for 20 minutes, until lightly golden. Break off the overhanging pastry. Leave the oven on.

Put the egg, sugar and flour in a bowl and use a whisk to beat until thick and pale. Put the butter in a small saucepan over medium heat. Leave to melt until frothy and dark golden, with a nutty aroma. Working quickly, pour the melted butter over the egg mixture and beat well.

Scatter the frozen raspberries in the tart case. Pour the warm batter over the raspberries. Bake in the oven for about 45 minutes, until the top resembles a golden meringue. Leave to cool for 30 minutes before serving. Cut into slices and serve with chilled cream if you like.

chocolate and *hazelnut* brownies

makes
9

100 g dark chocolate, broken into pieces

2 tablespoons milk

125 g sunflower margarine

200 g caster sugar

2 eggs, beaten

50 g cocoa powder

75 g self-raising flour

50 g shelled hazelnuts, chopped

a baking tin, 18 cm square, lightly greased and lined with greaseproof paper

Everyone loves chocolate brownies. These are a slightly healthier version because they use sunflower margarine instead of butter. They also include hazelnuts but you can of course use pecans or walnuts if you prefer. Serve the brownie squares as an afternoon treat, in a packed lunch, at parties or as a pudding with fresh raspberries.

Preheat the oven to 170°C (325°F) Gas 3.

Put the chocolate in a saucepan with the milk and heat gently, stirring, until the chocolate is melted and smooth. Remove the pan from the heat and leave to cool slightly.

Put the margarine and sugar in a large bowl and beat with a handheld electric whisk or a wooden spoon until the mixture is light and fluffy. Beat in the eggs a little at a time, beating well after each addition, until blended. Sift the cocoa powder into the egg mixture and stir gently until mixed. Pour in the melted chocolate and stir well.

Gently stir in the flour and hazelnuts – do not beat or overmix or the brownies will be dry. Spoon the mixture into the prepared tin and smooth the top. Bake in the preheated oven for about 25 minutes. To test if they are cooked, insert a skewer into the centre; it should come out almost clean with a slightly sticky feel.

Remove the brownies from the oven and leave to cool before cutting into squares. Store in an airtight container for up to 1 week, or wrap and freeze for up to 1 month.

baked *apples* and *pears*

Baked fruit is both easy on the cook and easy on the waistline. This recipe gives quantities for two servings to make it simple to increase as needed. These are really good served with a dollop of natural, unsweetened Greek yoghurt.

Preheat the oven to 200°C (400°F) Gas 6.

Peel the apples. If necessary, trim the bottoms slightly so that they sit flat. Using a small knife or a corer, remove the cores. With a small spoon, scrape out some apple around the core cavity to allow for more stuffing. Peel the pear, halve and scoop out the core, as for the apple.

In a small bowl, mix together the hazelnuts, sultanas and apricots.

Arrange the apples and pears in the baking dish. Stuff the nut mixture into the apple and pear cavities, mounding it on top. Top each with a light sprinkling of cinnamon and a good knob of butter, then drizzle each with 1–2 teaspoons of honey, to taste. Cover with foil.

Bake in the preheated oven for 20 minutes, then remove the foil and continue baking until just golden, about 10–15 minutes. Divide the apples and pears carefully between serving plates and pour over any pan juices. Serve warm with natural Greek yoghurt if you like.

serves
2

*baked apples
and pears*

2 apples, preferably Cox's or Braeburn

1 just-ripe pear, preferably Conference

20 g shelled hazelnuts, chopped

1 tablespoon sultanas

4–5 dried apricots, chopped

ground cinnamon, for dusting

about 50 g unsalted butter

runny honey, to drizzle

a non-stick baking dish, large enough to comfortably hold the fruit

desserts   **221**

summer *fruit* slice

This slice has a lovely fruity surprise sandwiched in the centre – a juicy layer of summer berries. Serve it in squares with an extra helping of berries. A scoop of vanilla ice cream is also delicious. If fresh berries are out of season, you can buy a bag of frozen fruit instead.

makes
16

250 g plain flour

200 g ground almonds

200 g unsalted butter, softened

200 g caster sugar

2 eggs, lightly beaten

300 g mixed summer berries, such as raspberries, strawberries and blackberries, plus extra to serve

a 20-cm square cake tin, greased and base-lined with greaseproof paper

Preheat the oven to 180°C (350°F) Gas 4.

Put the flour, almonds, butter, sugar and eggs in a mixing bowl and mix to a soft dough. Divide the mixture in half.

Press one half of the dough into the prepared tin. The easiest way to do this is to take a small handful of dough, flatten it slightly in your hand, then press it into the tin. Repeat to make an even layer about 1 cm thick.

Lightly press the summer berries into the dough in an even layer. Top the fruit with the remaining dough, covering it in an even layer using the method above.

Put the tin in the centre of the preheated oven and bake for 35–40 minutes until the top is light golden. Remove from the oven and transfer to a wire rack to cool for 10 minutes.

To remove the cake from the tin, put the wire rack on top of the tin and carefully turn it over so the rack is on the bottom – the cake should slide out of the tin. Peel away the greaseproof paper lining, then turn the cake over. Cut into 16 squares and serve with berries.

*rhubarb and
custard pots*

*baked
cheesecake*

rhubarb and *custard* pots

600 g rhubarb, trimmed and chopped into 3-cm pieces

3 tablespoons caster sugar

1 teaspoon grated orange zest

2 tablespoons orange juice

Custard

250 ml single cream

250 ml double cream

1 vanilla pod, split lengthways by running a small, sharp knife down the pod

4 egg yolks

2 tablespoons caster sugar

2 tablespoons flaked almonds, toasted in a dry frying pan

These are very pretty desserts, perfect for entertaining, as they can be made well in advance and popped in the fridge until you are ready to serve. Note that early forced rhubarb is more tender and will cook much more quickly than the later, ruby-coloured stalks. Keep your eye on it as it cooks. You don't want a pink mush, but rather a softly poached fruit that's still intact.

Put the rhubarb, sugar, orange zest and juice, and 2 tablespoons water in a saucepan over high heat. Cook, stirring constantly, until the mixture boils. Reduce the heat to medium and simmer for 5 minutes, until the rhubarb is soft but still retains some shape. Spoon the rhubarb into 6 individual serving dishes and set aside to cool while you make the custard.

Put both the single and double cream in a saucepan. Set over low heat and add the vanilla pod. Slowly bring the cream to the boil. As the cream boils, remove the pod and scrape the seeds into the custard, discarding the pod. Put the egg yolks and sugar in a bowl and whisk for 1 minute. Slowly pour the hot cream into the yolk mixture, whisking constantly. Transfer the mixture to a clean saucepan and set over low heat. Cook for 5 minutes, being careful not to let it boil until thickened.

While still warm, spoon the custard over the rhubarb and let the pots cool in the fridge for at least 3 hours or overnight before serving.

baked cheesecake

This is food to impress. Make it the day before you serve it and don't stress about cracks in the surface – they add character! For the best result, bring the cream cheese, eggs and soured cream to room temperature before using.

serves
10

Preheat the oven to 170°C (325°F) Gas 3. Wrap the entire outside of the prepared cake tin in 2 layers of foil.

Put the biscuits in a polythene bag and crush with a rolling pin. Pour into a bowl with 1 tablespoon of the sugar. Add the melted butter and mix until well combined. Tip the crumb mixture into the prepared tin and spread evenly over the base. Use the bottom of a glass tumbler to firmly press the crumb mixture into the tin. Bake in the preheated oven for 20 minutes (and leave the oven on). Remove and leave to cool completely.

Put the cream cheese and remaining sugar in a bowl and beat for about 2 minutes, until smooth and well combined. Add the eggs, one at a time, beating well between each addition and scraping down the side of the bowl. Add the lemon zest and soured cream. Beat until lump-free.

Pour the mixture into the prepared tin and level the top with a knife. Bake in the oven for 1 hour, until the top is golden but the centre is still wobbly. Turn the oven off and partially open the oven door. Let the cheesecake cool in the oven for 1 hour. Refrigerate for 6 hours, or ideally overnight.

Remove the cheesecake from the refrigerator 1 hour before eating. When ready to serve, run a warm, dry knife around the edge of the cake and remove the springform side. Cut into generous wedges.

160 g very dry, slightly sweet biscuits, such as Rich Tea

225 g caster sugar

100 g unsalted butter, melted

750 g cream cheese

5 eggs

1 teaspoon grated lemon zest

300 ml soured cream

a springform cake tin, 23 cm in diameter, lined with greaseproof paper and lightly greased

coconut caramel sauce

Coconut milk adds an exotic twist to caramel sauce, which makes the perfect addition to the Pan-fried Caribbean Bananas on page 227 or to char-grilled mango.

serves
4

Q

Heat all the ingredients in a small saucepan until the sugar dissolves. Bring to the boil and simmer for 8–10 minutes, or until the sauce is thick and glossy. Serve warm.

100 g dark brown soft sugar

100 g unsalted butter

175 ml coconut milk

almond and lemon cake

almond and *lemon* cake

Lemons and almonds are a flavour match made in heaven and they're divine here in this cake. It's the perfect no-fuss recipe for feeding a sweet-toothed crowd.

serves
10

Preheat the oven to 180°C (350°F) Gas 4.

Finely grate the zest from 2 of the lemons and squeeze all 3 of them so that you have 80 ml lemon juice. Put the butter, caster sugar and lemon zest in a bowl and, using a handheld electric whisk or a wooden spoon, beat for about 5 minutes, until the mixture is thick. Add the eggs, 1 at a time, and beat well between each addition. Fold in the flour, baking powder and ground almonds. Add the lemon juice and stir to combine. Spoon the mixture into the prepared tin and bake in the preheated oven for about 35 minutes, until the top of the cake is golden and the centre springs back when gently pressed. Remove from the tin and leave to cool.

To make the lemon icing, beat the icing sugar with the lemon juice for 2 minutes. Drizzle the icing over the cake and leave to set before serving.

3 lemons

200 g unsalted butter

200 g caster sugar

3 eggs

75 g plain flour

1 teaspoon baking powder

250 g ground almonds

Lemon icing

150 g icing sugar

2 tablespoons lemon juice

a 20-cm square cake tin, base-lined with greaseproof paper and lightly greased

pan-fried caribbean *bananas*

This dessert is superb topped with a dollop of crème fraîche or fromage frais, and perhaps a sprinkling of pumpkin seeds. It's super-quick, and quite healthy, so you don't need to feel guilty about having dessert after a big meal!

serves
2

Q

Melt the margarine and honey in a non-stick frying pan over high heat. Add the bananas and fry for 2–3 minutes until they are golden and softened.

Quickly stir in the sultanas, rum, if using, and orange juice. Bubble for about 30 seconds, then spoon into bowls and serve immediately.

1 tablespoon margarine

1 tablespoon runny honey

2 bananas, cut into 1-cm slices

25 g sultanas

1 tablespoon dark rum (optional)

juice of 1 small orange

ginger, rhubarb and cream cups

2–3 tablespoons runny honey

1–2 teaspoons ground ginger

400 g rhubarb, trimmed and chopped into 5-cm pieces

200 ml fromage frais or crème fraîche

25 g icing sugar

1 tablespoon grated lemon zest

The bite of the ginger and rhubarb against the mellowness of the cream makes this dessert irresistible. Eat it straight from a large bowl for a mid-week treat.

Put the honey, ground ginger and 200 ml water in a frying pan. Heat gently over medium heat and slowly bring to the boil, stirring occasionally. Reduce the heat and simmer for 10 minutes. Add the rhubarb to the pan and simmer for a further 8 minutes, until the rhubarb is soft but still retaining its shape. Remove the pan from the heat and leave to cool.

Drain the rhubarb, then divide it between 4 glasses. Refrigerate for 1 hour. Just before serving, put the fromage frais or crème fraîche, sugar and lemon zest in a bowl and mix. Spoon the mixture on top of the rhubarb.

strawberry tartlets

230 g plain flour

70 g icing sugar

170 g unsalted butter, chilled and cubed

2 large egg yolks

½ teaspoon vanilla extract

a little butter, for greasing

Strawberry topping

about 230 g redcurrant or raspberry jelly

about 500 g small strawberries, hulled

2 baking trays, greased

a pastry brush

These basic little tarts are made of a rich shortbread topped with small strawberries and a glossy, professional glaze.

Sift the flour and icing sugar into a mixing bowl. Add the butter and mix with your fingertips until it looks like fine breadcrumbs. Add the egg yolks and vanilla and mix until the dough comes together. Wrap the dough in clingfilm and refrigerate for 30 minutes.

Divide the dough into 6. Roll each piece into a ball and put on the prepared baking trays, setting them well apart. Press the dough to make circles about 7 mm thick. Pinch the edges with your fingers, then prick the bases all over with a fork. Refrigerate for 10 minutes.

Meanwhile, preheat the oven to 180°C (350°F) Gas 4.

Bake the circles in the preheated oven for 20 minutes until they are a light golden colour. Leave to cool on the trays.

To make the strawberry topping, put the jelly in a small saucepan with 1 tablespoon water and heat gently. Remove from the heat before it starts to boil. Set each cooked pastry circle on a plate. Using a pastry brush, brush a little hot jelly over each circle. Arrange the strawberries on the base and brush with the hot glaze. Leave until set – about 20 minutes – before serving.

strawberry tartlets

berries with
honeyed yoghurt

berries with *honeyed yoghurt*

Dessert doesn't get simpler than this. When you just have to satisfy a sweet, after-dinner craving but you don't want a full-blown pudding, try this. It's refreshing and delicious.

serves
4–6

Q

Reserve a few of the best berries for serving and put the remainder into a saucepan. Add the lemon zest, lemon juice, cinnamon and 1 tablespoon water. Heat gently for about 3 minutes until the berries just start to soften slightly. Leave to cool.

Spoon the berries into 4–6 glasses, then add the yoghurt and honey. Top with the reserved berries and serve.

200 g blueberries

a strip of lemon zest

a squeeze of lemon juice

a pinch of ground cinnamon

600 ml natural yoghurt

6 tablespoons runny honey

275 g very ripe strawberries, hulled

200 ml natural yoghurt

250 ml ready-made custard

½ teaspoon vanilla extract (optional)

6 amaretti biscuits, roughly broken

strawberry sundaes

 serves 2

 Q

Layers of fresh strawberry sauce and crushed amaretti biscuits are interspersed with creamy vanilla yoghurt custard to make a delicious dessert.

Set aside 4 strawberries to decorate. Purée the remaining fruit by pressing it through a sieve. Set aside.

Mix together the yoghurt, custard and vanilla extract, if using, in a bowl.

Spoon a layer of the yoghurt mixture into 2 tall glasses. Top with a layer of strawberry purée and amaretti biscuits. Repeat with another layer of yoghurt mixture, the remaining purée and amaretti. Top with a final layer of yoghurt mixture.

Slice the reserved strawberries and use to decorate the sundaes.

75 g caster sugar

2.5 cm fresh ginger, peeled and finely chopped

juice of ½ large lemon

1 large, ripe melon

melon with *ginger* syrup

 serves 4–6

 Q

Melon and ginger are a classic combination of flavours and this simple version is perfect for a warm summer's day. You can use any type of melon, but cantaloupe works particularly well.

Put the sugar and 150 ml water into a small saucepan and heat gently to dissolve the sugar. Bring to the boil, add the ginger and lemon juice and simmer gently for 3 minutes. Remove from the heat and leave to cool.

Cut the melon into wedges, scoop out the seeds and serve drizzled with ginger syrup.

strawberry sundaes

triple *chocolate* pancakes

Complete chocolate overload! These wicked little pancakes are packed with velvety melted chocolate and finished with the sweet and sour taste of smooth white chocolate yoghurt.

makes
12

285 g plain flour

75 g cocoa powder

1 teaspoon baking powder

1 teaspoon bicarbonate of soda

55 g caster sugar

200 ml milk

125 ml buttermilk

2 eggs, separated

30 g unsalted butter, melted and cooled

½ teaspoon salt

100 g dark chocolate, chopped

100 g white chocolate, chopped

Hot Chocolate Sauce (page 234), to serve

White chocolate yoghurt

150 g white chocolate, broken into pieces

4 tablespoons Greek yoghurt

Sift the flour, cocoa, baking powder, bicarbonate of soda and sugar into a bowl. Put the milk, buttermilk, egg yolks and cooled melted butter into a second large bowl and beat well. Add the flour mixture and mix thoroughly.

Put the egg whites and salt into a clean bowl and whisk with a handheld electric whisk until stiff peaks form. Add 1 tablespoon of the egg whites to the chocolate mixture and stir to loosen it, then carefully fold in the remaining egg whites, then the dark and white chocolate.

Heat a greased frying pan over medium heat. Reduce the heat. Pour about 2 tablespoons of batter into the pan and cook in batches of 3–4 over low heat for about 1 minute, or until small bubbles begin to appear on the surface and the underside is golden brown. Turn the pancakes over and cook the other side for 1 minute. Transfer to a plate and keep them warm in a low oven while you cook the remainder.

To make the white chocolate yoghurt, put the chocolate into a bowl set over a saucepan of simmering water and melt slowly. Do not let the base of the bowl touch the water. Remove from the heat and leave to cool a little, then beat in the yoghurt until smooth and shiny. Serve with the pancakes and Hot Chocolate Sauce.

scotch pancakes

100 g self-raising flour

a pinch of salt

1 egg

25 g caster sugar, plus extra
to serve

125 ml milk

40 g unsalted butter, plus
extra to serve

Scotch pancakes should be served warm, more or less straight from the pan, spread with butter and sprinkled with sugar.

Put the flour and salt in a large mixing bowl, make a dip in the centre and add the egg, sugar and milk. Melt 25 g of the butter in a small saucepan, then add to the mixing bowl. Work the mixture together with a whisk or wooden spoon to make a smooth batter. Beat for 1 minute, then set aside for 10 minutes.

Set a frying pan over medium heat, add the remaining butter and when it melts, swish it around the pan, then pour off the excess into a small heatproof bowl. Put the pan back on the heat and spoon 1 tablespoon of the batter into the pan. Cook until the pancake browns and bubbles appear on the surface, then turn it over. Transfer to a plate and keep it warm in a low oven while you cook the remainder. Return a little of the melted butter back to the pan as necessary. Serve immediately, spread with butter and sprinkled with caster sugar.

chocolate-dipped *fruit*

500 g fresh, ripe, but firm fruit, such as strawberries, apples, seedless grapes or satsumas

Hot chocolate sauce

100 g dark chocolate, broken into pieces

1 teaspoon golden syrup

*a few cocktail sticks or
skewers*

This is fun food – not very sophisticated (unless you stick to strawberries and dip them neatly into the chocolate) but all the better for it. There's something pleasing about healthy fruit smothered in irresistible melted chocolate.

Wash the fruit and dry it carefully with kitchen paper. Leave the small fruit whole. Cut the apples into thin wedges and remove the core. Divide the satsumas into segments.

Put the chocolate and golden syrup into a bowl set over a saucepan of simmering water and melt slowly. Do not let the base of the bowl touch the water. Heat gently, stirring occasionally, until the chocolate is melted and smooth. Remove the bowl from the heat and leave to cool slightly.

Pierce a piece of fruit with a cocktail stick or skewer and dip it into the melted chocolate. Transfer to a sheet of greaseproof paper and leave to set for about 1 hour. Eat within 3–4 hours of coating.

scotch pancakes

index

recipe credits

Nadia Arumugam
Stir-fried vegetables with
five-spice tofu

Fiona Beckett
Extra-crispy macaroni cheese
Mac 'n' greens

Vatcharin Bhumichitr
Egg noodles stir-fried with
vegetables and curry paste

Celia Brooks Brown
Char-grilled asparagus and leaf
salad with sesame-soy
dressing
Chilli greens with garlic crisps
Minty char-grilled courgettes
Pad Thai noodles
Thai coleslaw
Tomato and bread salad
Warm chickpea salad with
spiced mushrooms

Tamsin Burnett-Hall
Bean and vegetable soup
Mustardy mushroom stroganoff
Pan-fried Caribbean bananas

Maxine Clark
Asparagus with Parmesan and
chopped eggs
Aubergine, tomato and
Parmesan gratin
Belgian leek tart
Classic Italian salad
Grated cucumber, soured cream
and paprika salad
Mushroom risotto
Spinach risotto with rocket and
roasted tomatoes
Tomato, mozzarella and basil
salad

Linda Collister
Easy speedy pizza
Juicy fruit crisp
Strawberry tartlets
Tomato and red lentil soup

Ross Dobson
Almond and lemon cake
Asian-style tofu omelette
Asparagus, sweetcorn and
goats' cheese frittata
Baked cheesecake
Baked spinach mornay
Braised fennel with polenta
Broccoli and potato frittata
Cauliflower and caperberries on
halloumi
Cauliflower and Swiss chard
salad with chickpeas
Coconut creamed rice with
poached plums
Fresh tomato, pea and paneer
curry
Garden salad with garlic toasts
Mozzarella and basil toasties
Nectarine and pistachio crumble
Orange vegetable and spring
onion pilau
Pan plum crumble
Pasta with purple sprouting
broccoli, chilli and pine nuts
Pumpkin and Gorgonzola risotto
Pumpkin and feta parcels
Raspberry and almond tart
Rhubarb and custard pots
Roasted early autumn
vegetables with chickpeas
Smashed roast potatoes
Spaghetti with butternut squash,
sage and Pecorino
Spaghetti with peas and mint
Spiced aubergine couscous
Spinach and cheese curry
Stir-fried tofu with crisp greens
and mushrooms
Tabbouleh with chickpeas and
spring salad
Upside-down tomato tart
Wholemeal spaghetti with
courgettes and herbs

Clare Ferguson
Mixed vegetable tian
Penne with mozzarella, herbs
and tomatoes
Spaghetti with tomatoes and
aubergines

Urşula Ferrigno
Broccoli and lemon risotto
Country-style risotto
Farmers' risotto
Fennel and lemon risotto
Risotto with aubergine, pine nuts
and tomatoes
Risotto with lemon and mint
Tomato risotto

Liz Franklin
Big pasta shells stuffed with
herbs and ricotta
Creamy pea soup
Farfalle with courgettes,
sultanas and pine nuts
Penne with tomatoes and basil
Spaghetti with herbs and garlic

Manisha Gambhir Harkins
Aubergine and tomato stacks
Raw tomato and herb sauce on
grilled polenta
Warm goats' cheese salad

Tonia George
Huevos rancheros
Couscous with roast squash,
halloumi, dates and
pistachios
Omelette with chives and
cheese

Brian Glover
Squash and sage frittata

Nicola Graimes
Cottage cheese pancakes with
sweet chilli mushrooms
Courgette, potato and onion
tortilla
Lebanese halloumi salad
Lemon and spinach Puy lentils
with hard-boiled eggs
Soufflé cheese omelette
Strawberry sundaes
Summer fruit slice
Tofu and vegetable wraps

Kate Habershon
Triple chocolate pancakes

Rachael Anne Hill
Baked mushrooms
Chilli pasta bake
Chocolate and hazelnut
brownies
Chocolate-dipped fruit
Creamy spinach
Double chocolate fruity squares
Feta-stuffed peppers
Ginger, rhubarb and cream
cups
Home-made baked beans
Mozzarella-topped herby
vegetable loaf
Rice and bean burgers
Sesame sugar snap peas
Spicy lentil dip
Vegetable burritos
Warm potato salad

Caroline Marson
Lemon and herb feta salad
Roast tomato, goats' cheese and
rocket tartlets
Roasted butternut squash risotto
Roasted vegetable soup

Jane Noraika
Beef tomatoes with garlic and
herb butter
Feta salad with sugar snap peas
Portobello mushrooms with
lemon and olive oil
Thrown-together olives,
tomatoes and feta
Whole cauliflower with olives

Elsa Petersen-Schepelern
Baba ganoush
Chilli and mint raita
Cucumber and ginger raita
French onion soup
Stir-fried mushrooms
Tomato, onion and chilli raita

Louise Pickford
Avocado salsa
Baked goats' cheese on toast
Berries with honeyed yoghurt
Chunky aubergine burgers
Coconut caramel sauce
Curried sweet potato burgers
Farfalle with roasted squash,
feta and sage sauce
Melon with ginger syrup
Quick Mexican mole
Quick-vegetable curry
Scrambled eggs with
mushrooms
Spiced falafel burgers
Stir-fried tofu with chilli coconut
sauce
Tomato and olive tart with
Parmesan
White bean soup with olive
gremolata

Rena Salaman
Baked aubergines with garlic
and tomatoes
Courgette fritters

Jennie Shapter
Char-grilled pepper frittata
Feta, tomato and herb omelette
Indian omelette
Mushroom and pepper tortilla
Roasted vegetable tortilla
Sweet potato and Brie tortilla

Fiona Smith
Apple and bulghur wheat salad
Crushed peas
Olive oil and garlic bread
Portuguese potatoes
Ratatouille
Tomato, avocado and lime salad
with crisp tortillas

Sonia Stevenson
Roast butternut squash
Sweet potatoes skewers

Sunil Vijayakar
Cauliflower masala

Fran Warde
Avocado and chickpea salad
Baked fennel with shallots and
spicy dressing
Pappardelle with parsley
Poached mushrooms with egg
noodles
Warm Puy lentil salad

Laura Washburn
Apple coleslaw
Baked apples and pears
Greek omelette

Lindy Wildsmith
Black bean and avocado salad
Fusilli with tomatoey sauce
Lemon roast potato wedges
Linguine with ricotta, cinnamon
and walnuts
Pasta with basic cream, butter
and Parmesan sauce
Pasta with quick tomato sauce
Rigatoni with roasted vegetables
Scotch pancakes
Red kidney bean curry

photography credits

Key: a=above, b=below, r=right, l=left, c=centre.

Richard Jung
Pages 2, 8, 11ar, 31, 38, 39a, 39c,
40, 54, 57, 62, 63a, 68, 82, 85,
86, 97, 106, 109, 114, 125, 129,
130, 167, 168, 175b, 179, 183,
187, 198, 204, 210, 211a, 215,
216, 224l, 226

Peter Cassidy
Pages 11al, 12-13bc, 13b, 16,
17b, 21, 47, 75, 87a, 91, 93r,
105a, 111r, 113, 117, 126, 134,
174, 184, 203, 207, 221

Martin Brigdale
Pages 3c, 12-13a, 35, 71, 138, 142,
157, 158, 175c, 176, 208, 235

Tara Fisher
Pages 1, 11bl, 15, 87b, 94, 105b,
153, 162, 165, 171, 195, 197

Nicki Dowey
Pages 11br, 18, 72, 76, 81, 98, 149,
154, 175a, 180

Diana Miller
Pages 3l, 13a, 32, 39b, 43, 44, 48,
51, 104, 122

William Reavell
Pages 3r, 5, 53, 87c, 88, 101, 121,
200, 222, 231

Jason Lowe
Pages 133, 137, 141, 145, 146,
188, 191

Lisa Linder
Pages 14, 63c, 63b, 64, 67, 79

William Lingwood
Pages 17a, 22, 261, 28, 232

Kate Whitaker
Pages 118, 211c, 211b, 219, 224r

Vanessa Davies
Pages 93l, 172, 212, 229l

Philip Webb
Pages 17c, 25, 37, 58

Jean Cazals
Pages 61, 102, 192

David Munns
Pages 12bl, 105c, 161

Jonathan Gregson
Pages 6, 151

Jeremy Hopley
Page 111l

Debi Treloar
Page 26r

Ian Wallace
Page 229l